# MAPPING THE MARKETS

OTHER ECONOMIST BOOKS

Guide to Analysing Companies
Guide to Business Modelling
Guide to Business Planning
Guide to Economic Indicators
Guide to the European Union
Guide to Financial Markets
Guide to Investment Strategy
Guide to Management Ideas
Numbers Guide
Style Guide

Dictionary of Business
Dictionary of Economics
International Dictionary of Finance

Brands and Branding
Business Consulting
Business Ethics
Business Miscellany
Business Strategy
China's Stockmarket
Dealing with Financial Risk
Economics
Future of Technology
Globalisation
Headhunters and How to Use Them
Successful Mergers
The City
Wall Street

Essential Director
Essential Economics
Essential Investment
Essential Negotiation

# MAPPING THE MARKETS

## A Guide to Stockmarket Analysis

**Deborah Owen**
**Robin Griffiths**

BLOOMBERG PRESS

NEW YORK

THE ECONOMIST IN ASSOCIATION WITH
PROFILE BOOKS LTD

Published in the United States and Canada by Bloomberg Press
Published in the U.K. by Profile Books Ltd, 2006

Printed in the United Kingdom
1 3 5 7 9 10 8 6 4 2
Library of Congress Cataloging-in-Publication Data

Owen, Deborah.
   Mapping the markets : a guide to stockmarket analysis / by Deborah Owen & Robin Griffiths.
      p. cm.
   Summary: "This book is about how to analyze the way markets are likely to behave. It combines technical analysis, which is based on the belief that price reflects everything that is known about a particular market, and fundamental analysis, which takes into account an individual company's sales, earnings, and the value of its assets"--Provided by publisher.
Includes bibliographical references and index.
   ISBN-13: 978- 1-57660-238-6 (alk. paper)
   ISBN-10: 1-57660-238-9
   1. Stock exchanges. 2. Business cycles. 3. Investments. I. Griffiths, Robin II. Title.

HG4551 . O94 2006
332.63'22--dc22                                                    2006024285

For our respective children

# Contents

# List of figures

## List of tables

# Acknowledgements

W e would like to acknowledge the input of our colleagues Richard Marshall of Investment Research of Cambridge and Rashpal Sohan of Rathbones in producing this book. Richard Marshall not only found many of the examples shown but also read through the manuscript and made constructive comments.

A much appreciated source of help with financial statistics and market data has been Les Curtis of Thomson Financial. We are grateful to him for his advice and suggestions and to Thomson Financial for permission to reproduce some of their data. We would also like to thank Peter Cole and Richard Guy for their comments on the first draft.

In our analysis of economic and stockmarket cycles, we have relied on primary research of other analysts and drawn together a broad spread of subjects. We do not profess to be experts in all these areas and are immensely grateful to the authors whose works are acknowledged in the bibliography. In addition, we would like to thank Christopher Watson, of The Pugwash Organisation (an NGO committed to the beneficial application of new developments in science and technology), for his helpful comments on the energy section. We are indebted to Clive Cookson not only for his excellent coverage of scientific developments in the *Financial Times* but also for reading through the section on biotechnology. Kenneth Owen provided helpful input on medical innovations. It would have been impossible to do any background research in Beijing without the friendly and knowledgeable assistance of Shelagh and Mike Timberley and the inestimable Mr Sun. We do, however, take full responsibility for any mistakes that appear.

Finally, we would like to thank Stephen Brough of Profile Books for his patience and encouragement and Penny Williams for her expert copy-editing.

# Introduction

The global financial markets turn over billions of dollars daily. An array of different instruments is available to trade in these markets, ranging from the relatively simple purchase of a stock to trading such exotic creatures as butterfly spreads. Participation at any level involves taking a view as to which way the market in question will move. There are essentially only two methods for analysing the future direction of any market, whether it be equities, currencies, interest rates or commodities: one involves fundamental analysis, the other technical analysis.

Fundamental analysts weigh up all the relevant economic variables and then make a judgment as to whether the current price of a share or market represents what they have calculated to be "fair" value or whether it is overvalued or undervalued compared with what they perceive to be the "correct" level. Technical analysts believe that, at any particular time, the price reflects everything that is known about a market or stock. Furthermore, since markets essentially reflect human behaviour and since human behaviour is broadly consistent over time, there is a tendency for price behaviour to follow similar patterns. Prices, therefore, move within trends which appear more often and persist for longer than the laws of chance would allow.

Fundamental and technical analysts occupy two camps which are separated by a wide gulf. Few analysts straddle this gulf and what interchange there is between the two camps can be adversarial. Technical analysts are often perceived by economists as having a "mystic" tendency while, from the other side of the divide, fundamental analysts are thought to be detached from the real world as, for example, when just one month before the onset of the 1990 US recession, a group of economists put out a joint statement ruling out any downturn for at least one to three years. Essentially this hostility reflects a lack of understanding about the strengths and weaknesses inherent in both types of analysis. Technical analysis has a good track record in predicting market outcomes, although some of those involved in the financial markets remain unconvinced by the methodology in the mistaken belief that it lacks analytical rigour. Fundamental analysis, however, is useful in gauging what is happening in an economy (and therefore in explaining what is driving the trends that technical analysts are watching), but it has always been slow to pick up turning points.

The mutual suspicion between technical and fundamental analysts belies the fact that both forms of analysis are rooted in cycle theory. The business cycle is an integral part of economic analysis, and a belief in the cyclical nature of markets is a central plank of technical analysis. Cycle analysis is, therefore, the interface between fundamental and technical analysis.

This book aims to explain not only how cycle theory links the disciplines of fundamental analysis and technical analysis, but also how cycle theory can be used to navigate successfully through the changing global economic landscape.

At the 2006 World Economic Forum meeting in Davos, Larry Summers, then president of Harvard University, suggested that increasing globalisation and technological change represent the third great economic wave in human history. The two previous waves occurred during the Renaissance and the Industrial Revolution. Economic tidal waves of this nature take a long time to build up and the Technology Revolution is still at the groundswell stage. As it gathers momentum, it will give rise to the sort of investment opportunities that occur not just once in a lifetime but once in a century. An understanding of how cycles work will help investors anticipate the market trends emanating from this economic tidal wave. Knowing the whereabouts of a market in relation to the cycle is an essential piece of information not just for the long-term buy-and-hold investor but also for the very short-term day trader.

This book is in four parts, summarised below.

## Part 1 Tools for mapping the markets

Business cycles provide the underlying propulsion for both the economy and the stockmarket. An understanding of what causes shifts in both the trend and the intensity of this underlying force is a key element in the successful prediction of market outcomes.

In pre-industrial times, the ebbs and flows of an economy were tied to crops. Once manufactured goods started to account for an increasingly large share of a country's annual gross domestic product, it might have been supposed that the regular output from a factory would translate into a fairly steady rise in economic growth, but this did not happen. In the 19th century, economists started investigating what caused the regular periods of economic expansion and contraction that they observed.

In the early part of the 20th century, a Russian economist, Nikolai Kondratieff, identified a very long cycle of 50–60 years inherent in the western economies. A few decades earlier, a British economist, William

Jevons, and a French economist, Clement Juglar, had independently picked up on an economic oscillation that occurred approximately every decade. In the 1920s, two Harvard professors, W.L. Crum and Joseph Kitchin, separately identified a much shorter 40-month cycle in interest rates. One of the most distinguished economists of the 20th century, Joseph Schumpeter, knitted these cycles together to form a "three-cycle schema". And it is this that provides the bedrock of cycle analysis. Chapter 1 explains the relative importance of these three cycles from the perspective of an investor.

The relationship between the economy and the stockmarket is analysed in Chapter 2. By linking economic cycles to the stockmarket, a series of "road maps" can be constructed which will enable investors to identify which global markets are likely to show outperformance.

At different points in the cycle, different sectors of the market will outperform. The concept of sector rotation is explained in Chapter 3.

When it comes to day-to-day investment decisions, such as when to enter or exit a position or which stocks to buy, a more detailed reading of the market is required. The tools of technical analysis pick up on the forces of supply and demand within any particular market. Although this book is not intended to be a technical analysis primer, Chapter 4 examines some of the techniques that can be used to identify trends and "read" the chart of a share price from a technical perspective.

## Part 2 Long-term cyclical drivers

Economic waves are triggered by technological change. Gutenberg's invention of the printed book was the catalyst for the Renaissance. It allowed literature, art, philosophy and science to become much more widely disseminated. At around the same time, Vasco de Gama's discovery of the sea route to India sparked off a huge rise in world trade.

It is harder to identify one particular innovation that triggered the move to greater mechanisation during the Industrial Revolution, but a strong contender for the title of "chief catalyst" must be James Watt's refinement of the steam engine. His adjustments to Thomas Newcomen's engine allowed a great variety of machines to be powered by the steam engine. There was some delay before this new technology ushered in completely new systems of transport – canals, railways and steamships – because a way had to be found to mechanise the production of coal. But eventually the mining industry was able to produce coal on a sufficiently large scale to initiate another huge surge in global trade using these new forms of transport.

The trigger for what Summers describes as the third wave of economic advancement has been rapid changes in technology and the introduction of the internet. These have brought down the cost of communications, as well as that of storing and processing information. This is paving the way for the industrialisation of not just China and India but also many other countries. In the world of science, the decoding of the human genome is a breakthrough discovery that has opened up whole new branches of biotechnology and computer sciences. Chapters 5–8 investigate some of the themes that are likely to drive this new economic wave.

## Part 3 Downward phases of the cycle

No trend or wave moves in a straight line, so even against a broadly positive economic backdrop there will periods of downturn in both the economy and stockmarkets. Chapters 9 and 10 look at factors that could precipitate a downturn.

## Part 4 Taking market bearings

The final part of the book shows how cycle theory can be used to anticipate which markets and sectors will benefit from the changing economic landscape in the coming years. This is not intended to be a precise prediction of where any one market will be at any one time in the future but rather a broad indication of trend.

# PART 1
## TOOLS FOR MAPPING THE MARKETS

Cycle analysis provides investors with a compass reading of the whereabouts of the global markets. This is essential information which they need before they can begin to decide on the appropriate allocation of assets – equities, bonds, cash and other investments – within their portfolios. It also helps to determine geographic weighting. By setting stock selection within the context of cycle analysis, investors will know whether it is appropriate to chase momentum or pursue a more defensive strategy. Technical analysis identifies shares that are exhibiting the strongest upward momentum.

# 1 Economic cycles

At the heart of analysing market trends is the business cycle. It has long been appreciated that economies do not grow in a steady, linear direction; instead there are periods of expansion and contraction which tend to occur at regular intervals. Even in Genesis, the first book of the Bible, there is reference to seven lean years and seven years of plenty.

In pre-industrial times the phenomenon of economic fluctuations was tied to the agricultural cycle with crop failure causing severe hardship in agrarian-based economies. But as society became more industrialised, these cycles still persisted. John Bates Clark, an American economist writing at the end of the 18th century, said of them: "The modern world regards business cycles much as the ancient Egyptians regarded the overflowing of the Nile. The phenomenon recurs at intervals, it is of great importance to everyone and natural causes of it are not in sight." Society remained mystified by economic ebbs and flows until in the second half of the 19th century economists analysing statistical data noticed there was a periodic rhythm to these ups and downs.

## Historical analysis of the business cycle

One of the earliest investigations into patterns of economic activity was carried out in the 1880s by William Stanley Jevons, an economist, best known for his book *The Theory of Political Economy*. In a paper "The Periodicity of Commercial Crises and its Physical Explanation" published posthumously by H.S. Foxwell, Jevons noted that going back to the beginning of the 18th century, what he described as "commercial crises" occurred approximately every 9–12 years, with the average interval being 10.44 years. Although Jevons did not "believe that any of our economists have yet untied this Gordian knot of economic science", he thought the cause of these crises was linked to the cycle of sunspot activity on harvests.

At around the same time a French economist, Clement Juglar, discovered from his analysis of movements in interest rates and prices in the 1860s that alternating periods of prosperity and liquidation recurred on average every 9–10 years. However, it was a German economist, Werner Sombart, who first put forward the idea that these economic fluctuations should not be seen as a series of periodic crises but rather as a continuous wave that followed a set pattern of boom and bust. In the United States,

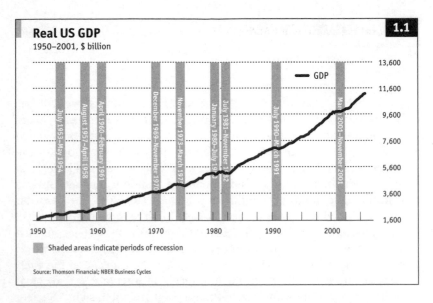

**Real US GDP**
1950–2001, $ billion

1.1

Shaded areas indicate periods of recession

Source: Thomson Financial; NBER Business Cycles

the approximately ten-year economic rhythm has continued almost unbroken throughout the 20th century. The year in which the downturn starts varies a little, but for the past half century it has always been in the first three years of the decade. Recessions can occur at other times in a decade, but there is no regular pattern – they may be the result of excessive policy adjustments or external economic shocks. So the approximately ten-year economic pulse which Jevons and Juglar identified in the 19th century still appears to be beating regularly.

## The long-term Kondratieff cycle

Working in the early years of the communist revolution, Nikolai Kondratieff, a Russian economist, was given the job of analysing the major capitalist economies – Germany, France, Britain and the United States – with a view to confirming the Marxist theory that capitalism contains the seeds of its own destruction. (Much of Kondratieff's work is based on Britain and France because before the mid-19th century these countries have "the most systematic statistical material".) After analysing statistics on commodity prices, interest rates, wages, foreign trade and production of coal, pig iron and lead going back to the late 18th century, he came to the conclusion that long-term fluctuations were an inherent feature of the capitalist system. So although downturns would occur, they would eventually always be followed by periods of economic recovery, and

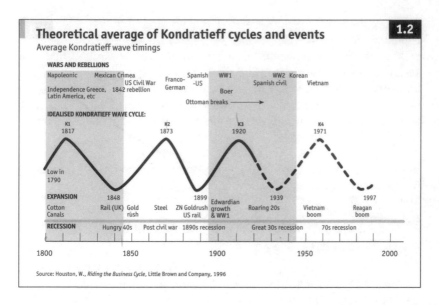

**Theoretical average of Kondratieff cycles and events** `1.2`
Average Kondratieff wave timings

Source: Houston, W., *Riding the Business Cycle*, Little Brown and Company, 1996

these waves would last for approximately 50–60 years from trough to trough (a duration of 54 years is usually quoted but this is simply the average of the first two long waves). Kondratieff anticipated that the length of each cycle would vary considerably. The first wave he identi-fied was from 1789 to 1849, the second was from 1849 to 1896 and the third he dated from 1896 and predicted would end in the 1930s. He therefore accurately anticipated the 1930s slump and the subsequent recovery.

Kondratieff also made some empirical observations associated with these waves. The first was that before the upward phase of each wave a significant number of technical innovations and discoveries occurred. He also noted that what he described as big "social upheavals and radical changes in the life of society (revolutions, wars)" were more likely to occur during the upward phase of the long cycle. As can be seen in Figure 1.2, the French Revolution, the Franco-Prussian war and the first world war all occurred during the rising phase of the cycle. His third observation was that the downward phase of the cycle coincided with periods of depres-sion in agriculture. Lastly, intermediate cycles of between seven and eleven years occurred within the long wave. Kondratieff did not suggest a causal connection between these observations or that they could in any way explain the existence of the long wave. He admitted that he could not give a satisfactory explanation as to what triggered economic upturns, but postulated that they might be related to the period of time that it took for capital equipment to wear out and be replaced.

Kondratieff's theory about long economic waves was published in a series of papers between 1922 and 1928. The idea that capitalism contained an economic "self-righting" mechanism ran counter to the views of the recently formed communist government and Kondratieff was put on trial. (Alexander Solzhenitsyn records in his book *The Gulag Archipelago* that Kondratieff was sentenced to solitary confinement, became mentally ill and died in prison.) His work was, however, smuggled out of Russia and published in Germany in 1926. An abridged English translation appeared in *The Quarterly Journal of Economics* in 1935.

### A milder Kondratieff down-wave?

It has been suggested that the down-waves of the very long-term Kondratieff cycle are becoming milder as financial authorities become better at registering and reacting to changing economic conditions. Other factors such as a shortening of the period between discovery and the commercial development of new ideas may also have a influence on this. Both Kondratieff and Schumpeter acknowledged the evolutionary aspect of economic trends. It is, however, premature to make any firm assumptions about the downward phase of the Kondratieff wave. Global imbalances such as the size of the US current account deficit and the huge rise in household debt in the Anglo-Saxon economies would, if they were to revert to more average levels over a short space of time, exert an extremely strong contractionary force on the world economy.

### The shorter-term Kitchin wave

Subsequently, a number of other economic waves were identified. In the early 1920s W.L. Crum, a Harvard professor, identified a cycle of around 40 months in commercial paper rates in New York. A little later Joseph Kitchin, another Harvard professor, also picked up a 40-month economic rhythm from his work analysing US and UK statistical data from 1890 to 1922. The Kitchin cycle was originally thought to reflect the stocking/destocking inventory cycle that companies went through, but computer technology has considerably dampened down the amplitude of the swings in inventory levels and therefore lessened their impact on the business cycle. This shorter cycle has now come to be associated with the

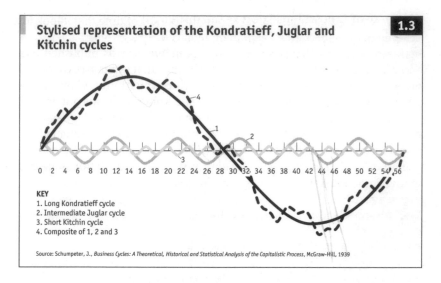

**Stylised representation of the Kondratieff, Juglar and Kitchin cycles**

1.3

KEY
1. Long Kondratieff cycle
2. Intermediate Juglar cycle
3. Short Kitchin cycle
4. Composite of 1, 2 and 3

Source: Schumpeter, J., *Business Cycles: A Theoretical, Historical and Statistical Analysis of the Capitalistic Process*, McGraw-Hill, 1939

economic swings linked to the US presidential election cycle (see page 17) and, as a result, is taken to have a span of four years.

### Schumpeter's three-cycle schema

By the early 1930s a number of different business cycles had been identified but no attempt had been made to see if there was any relationship between them. This task was undertaken by one of the great economists of the 20th century, an Austrian-born Harvard professor, Joseph Schumpeter. He investigated just three cycles: the Kondratieff, the Juglar and the Kitchin (Schumpeter emphasised that this did not imply that other cycles were any less valid but just that he had decided to focus on these three).

In 1939 Schumpeter published a two-volume work, *Business Cycles: A Theoretical, Historical and Statistical Analysis of the Capitalist Process*. In it he argued that his "three-cycle schema" were harmonics of each other. A Kondratieff wave would, therefore, contain five or six Juglars. Each Juglar wave would, in turn, consist of three or four Kitchins. Schumpeter acknowledged that the periodicity of these waves was not rigid and that the number of Kitchin waves in a Juglar or Juglar waves in a Kondratieff would not always be the same. But if the downward curve of each wave were in phase, the nadir of each would coincide, producing severe economic slumps or even depressions.

11

### "Clusters of innovations" power the uptrend

Schumpeter put forward an explanation as to why economies alternated between periods of contraction and expansion. The latter, he argued, occur because innovations happen in "clusters" as entrepreneurs are only prepared to take the business risk of launching their products commercially when economic conditions are favourable. In some cases one innovation can spark off others. For example, the ability to roll steel rails encouraged the growth of railways and this, in turn, made transport across the United States easier in the mid-19th century.

Kondratieff's long waves coincided with bursts of discoveries and innovations: the 1789 wave covered the first Industrial Revolution; the 1849 wave ushered in the era of steam and steel; and the post-1896 period saw the introduction of electricity, the internal combustion engine and many chemical discoveries. It is these clusters of innovation that power the upward phase of the long-term cycle.

### The positive effects of "creative destruction"

Schumpeter also analysed how resources move from older, less productive sectors of the economy into new, more dynamic industries. When a company goes bankrupt it is a tragedy for the people directly involved in the business – employees lose their jobs and shareholders lose the money they have invested – but it is an essential part of the capitalist system. Capital and labour tied up in inefficient companies are not being used to their full economic potential, so when a business collapses they can be released and reharnessed in a more productive sector of the economy – which is likely to be involved in the commercial development of innovations. It is this process that gives the market system its dynamism and is what Schumpeter described as "creative destruction".

### What is a cycle?

Figure 1.3 on page 11 shows the Kondratieff, Juglar and Kitchin cycles as smooth sine waves. (These are waves that look like the letter S tipped horizontally and linked to other Ss.) However, economists have an incomplete understanding of the shape and pattern of economic cycles. As Mervyn King, governor of the Bank of England, put it: "At school, we used to plot sine curves ... well, whatever the economic cycle is, it certainly isn't a sine curve." Schumpeter made the point that although business cycles can help to interpret "the general pattern of economic life", they do not replicate each other exactly but instead display a family likeness.

It is helpful for investors to know that, as far as the United States is

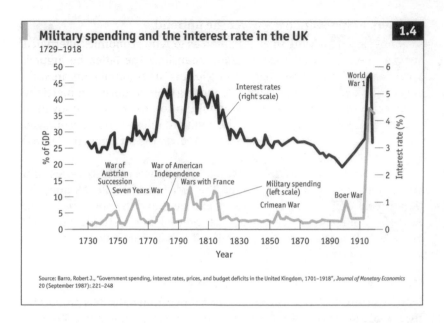

**Military spending and the interest rate in the UK**
1729–1918

1.4

Source: Barro, Robert J., "Government spending, interest rates, prices, and budget deficits in the United Kingdom, 1701–1918", *Journal of Monetary Economics* 20 (September 1987): 221–248

concerned, four-year and ten-year rhythms occur with remarkable regularity. When it comes to identifying major global trends, the much longer Kondratieff cycle is not particularly useful; Kondratieff thought the span of each cycle could vary by as much as 25% (the difference between the

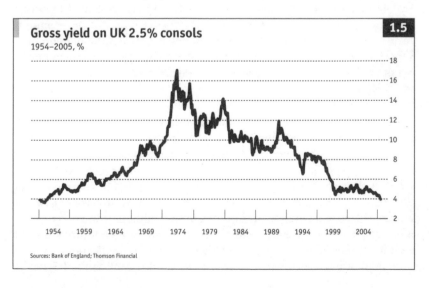

**Gross yield on UK 2.5% consols**
1954–2005, %

1.5

Sources: Bank of England; Thomson Financial

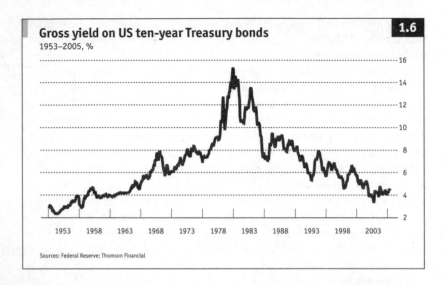

**Gross yield on US ten-year Treasury bonds**
1953–2005, %

1.6

Sources: Federal Reserve; Thomson Financial

lengths of the first two cycles he identified). A margin of error of this magnitude makes the Kondratieff cycle a very imprecise tool for market analysis. However, this does not mean that the idea of long-term cycles – which can exert either a negative or a positive pull on the economy and the markets – should be rejected. As can be seen in Figures 1.4, 1.5 and 1.6 (and in Figures 12.1 and 12.2 on pages 117 and 118), markets do trace out long-term cycles. Robert Barro, Paul M. Warburg Professor of Economics at Harvard University, has correlated interest rates with military spending in the UK. More recently, nominal long-term US and UK interest rates have traced out a 50-year cycle, reflecting the rise and fall of inflationary pressures. (Although it is the real rate of return that matters in terms of the underlying economy, the cycle of nominal rates is nevertheless important in determining asset allocation.)

From the perspective of a stockmarket investor it is more effective to focus on readily identifiable long-term "themes" that are likely to affect economic growth and which are known as secular trends.

## Secular trends

Secular trends are long-term trends that reflect economic and social changes in society and usually last for a generation or longer. Schumpeter identified the power that clusters of new innovations and technology had on the long-term economic cycle. It is, however, only lifestyle-changing innovations that have the power to affect long-term growth. The telephone and car are two such examples. More recently, it is advances in communication technology that are providing the spur for the next phase of industrialisation, itself the most powerful trigger for global growth.

Demographic trends are another secular factor that can have a powerful impact on the compound rate of growth of a country. The world is in the middle of a huge demographic transition that will have a significant effect on long-term economic trends. (In the 1930s, when Schumpeter was writing about business cycles, the powerful economic forces – industrialisation and demographics – were not considered variables. The process of industrialisation had already occurred in Europe and the United States, and even those with the foresight to envisage that industrialisation would spread to other parts of the world would have regarded it as too distant a prospect to be factored into economic cycle theory. Demographics were also considered a constant because before 1900 the growth of the world's population had been slow and, although life expectancy started to rise in the first half of the 20th century, few – if any – predicted the huge shifts in demographic trends that have subsequently occurred.)

The four-year and ten-year economic cycles can be skewed either upwards or downwards according to the pull that is being exerted on them by the underlying direction of the secular trend.

# 2 Stockmarket cycles

The cycles described in Chapter 1 are economic, but there is a simple link between the underlying economy and the stockmarket. The most consistent long-term driver of stock values is corporate earnings and the main determinant of these earnings is the business cycle. (There are times such as the dotcom boom of the late 1990s when the market pays scant regard to corporate earnings, but most of the time they are the crucial element.) The stockmarket, however, does not move exactly in step with the economy; it tends to look ahead and discount underlying changes in the economy so shares usually rise ahead of a recovery and fall before a recession. The market leads the economy by approximately six months, but the lead time can vary considerably. There is a further catch. Markets are made up of crowds of people who tend to act as a herd which is subject to severe mood swings – both to the upside and to the downside. These swings have a tendency to go too far. In this respect the stock-market is rather like a pendulum. If the pendulum stopped swinging, it would hang straight down. In practice, however, it spends a minimum amount of time in that position; most of the time it is swinging from left to right and back again. (See Part 4, page 101, for a more detailed analysis of the factors linking the economy and the stockmarket.) So it is with the stockmarket: market sentiment is either far too optimistic or far too pessimistic. Sometimes the market discounts economic events that do not happen. As Paul Samuelson, a Nobel Prize-winning economist, famously remarked: "The stockmarket has predicted nine out of the last five recessions."

As far as the stockmarket is concerned, the most important cycle is the four-year one. It has become locked in with the US presidential election cycle and, obviously, has the most direct bearing on the US stockmarket. But since the US stockmarket generally sets the trend for the rest of the world's markets, correctly predicting the direction of this market provides a useful guide to the broad trend of other global equity markets. The most obvious exception is Japan (see box on the next page).

## Japan in the doldrums

The Japanese stockmarket reached a peak of 39,000 on the Nikkei 225 Index in December 1989 and then experienced a 15-year bear market, hitting a low of 7,608 in April 2003. The bursting of the asset-price bubble in Japan revealed the weakness of the banking sector. Many companies and banks had cross-holdings in each other's shares which meant that there was a general reluctance to force companies into bankruptcy. Rather than let ailing companies go under, non-performing loans were frequently rolled over. As discussed in Chapter 1, "creative destruction" is an important part of the market system but this process had ceased to operate in Japan in the 1990s. Eventually, the authorities realised that "kindness" to the corporate sector was effectively killing the economy, and the first signs of a change in policy occurred in 1997 when three large financial institutions were allowed to go bankrupt. Although cross-holdings are gradually being unwound and bankruptcy is becoming a more regular feature of Japanese corporate life, unblocking the logjam of underperforming companies trapped in the less-efficient sectors of the economy will be a protracted process.

## The four-year cycle

The year before a US presidential election is usually a good one for the stockmarket. The uptrend continues during the year of the election and the new president is then given a short honeymoon period during his first year. It is not hard to find the reason for this. Halfway through his term of office the president begins to focus on his re-election (or ensuring his party stays in office if he is a second-term president). The most important influence on the electorate's voting behaviour is how they perceive their economic well-being. So in the run-up to an election everything possible is done to boost the economy. Once the president is re-elected, there is usually a reality check – a reining back of the budget deficit and a couple of years of fiscal restraint. This economic manipulation is reflected in the stockmarket's performance.

Some analysts question this rationale for the four-year cycle. Jeremy Grantham, an American fund manager, offers a more subtle explanation. Investors unconsciously believe that if anything were to happen to derail the stockmarket in the run-up to an election, the administration and perhaps also the Federal Reserve would step in with appropriate measures. Confidence that the authorities would bail out the stockmarket

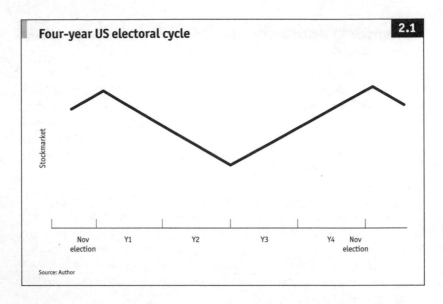

**Four-year US electoral cycle**    `2.1`

Stockmarket

Nov
election    Y1    Y2    Y3    Y4    Nov
election

Source: Author

if it ran into problems became known as the "Greenspan put" (after Alan Greenspan, former head of the Fed). Armed with this assurance, Grantham argues that investors usually buy aggressively ahead of a US presidential election.

Whatever the mechanics behind the four-year cycle, there is a marked difference between the performance of the stockmarket in the first two years of an administration and that of the second two years. According to *The Stock Trader's Almanac*, the last two years of the 43 administrations since 1833 have produced cumulative gains in the Dow Jones Industrial Average (based on Cowles and other indices before 1896) of 743% compared with gains of 228% in the first two years of these administrations. Over this period the average gain over the pre-election and election years is 17% a year compared with 5% a year in the post-election and mid-term years. This four-year pattern is shown in Figure 2.1.

### Seasonal trends

Another regular feature in stockmarkets is the seasonal trends. There is usually a strong run-up to the end of the year which can continue through to January. Often this is followed by a period of consolidation or even a correction before the market pushes higher again until May, when it is surprising how often the old adage "sell in May and go away" proves correct. After a lull over the summer months, trading activity picks up

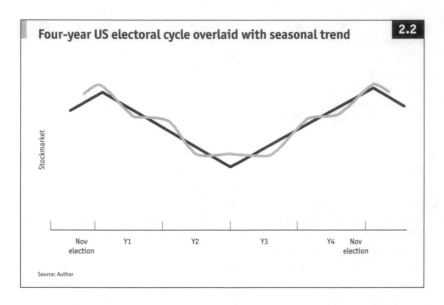

**2.2**

**Four-year US electoral cycle overlaid with seasonal trend**

Stockmarket

Nov election | Y1 | Y2 | Y3 | Y4 | Nov election

Source: Author

again and there can sometimes be a short rally, but investors tend to be constrained by the prospect of the autumnal squalls which regularly buffet stockmarkets during September and October. Once safely through the autumn, investors settle into the end-of-year rally. This seasonal pattern can be laid over the four-year cycle as shown in Figure 2.2.

### Autumn squalls

The autumn crash has become embedded in market psychology. The October falls in 1929 and 1987 may be the best-known crashes, but in six of the years between 1991 and 2005 the stockmarket has dropped significantly in either September or October, although some of the falls can be said to be squalls rather than full-blown crashes. There is even some speculation that the terrorist attacks on New York and Washington that took place on September 11th 2001 were planned partly to achieve the maximum financial disruption because of the market's known fragility during the autumn period. The usual explanation put forward to explain the falls which occur at this time of the year is that on returning from their summer vacations, fund managers and individual investors review their portfolios, and if they are showing healthy profits on the year so far they are tempted to take them. This might have been true some time ago, when most people took their annual leave at the same time over the summer, but nowadays holidays are much more spread out. It is more

19

probable that there is a self-fulfilling aspect to the autumn squall. Investors have September and October marked down as high-risk months, so if a small sell-off does occur – which at other times of the year might be ignored or even viewed as a buying opportunity – they rush to sell. As a result an almost Pavlovian response to selling pressure develops during these months.

The immediate question that arises from this simple four-year cycle is how do markets develop multi-year trends if they rally for two years and then give up much of their gains in the next two years? The first point to make is that despite the experience since 1990, markets do spend a lot of time moving broadly sideways. In the UK, for example, after shares peaked in 1968 they did not regain their value in real terms until May 1987.

When multi-year trends do emerge, such as in the long bull market seen in the United States during the 1980s and 1990s or the bear market experienced by Japanese investors in the 1990s, it is because longer-term trends are exerting a powerful "tidal pull" on the four-year cycle, which skews it either upwards or downwards (see Figures 2.3 and 2.4).

The four-year cycle is seen even more clearly when the stockmarket performance is shown in real terms (that is, adjusted for changes in the rate of inflation), as in Figure 2.5.

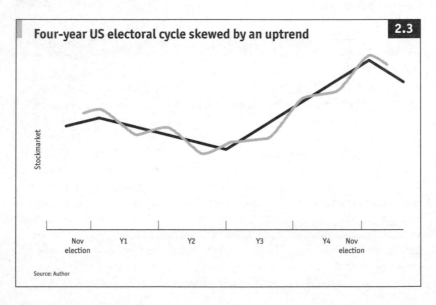

**Four-year US electoral cycle skewed by an uptrend**    **2.3**

Stockmarket

Nov election    Y1    Y2    Y3    Y4   Nov election

Source: Author

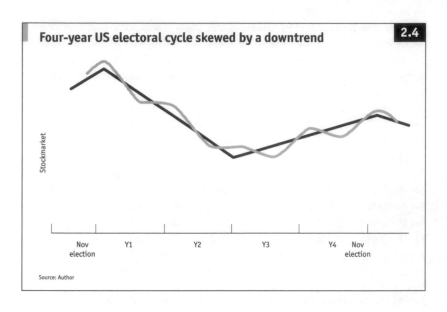

**Four-year US electoral cycle skewed by a downtrend** 2.4

Stockmarket

Nov election | Y1 | Y2 | Y3 | Y4 Nov election

Source: Author

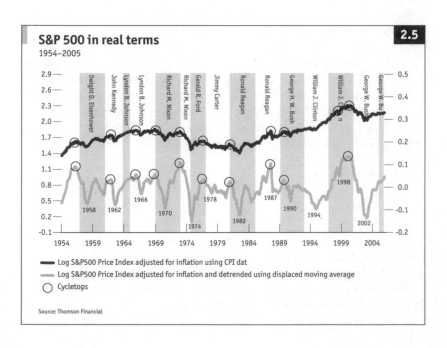

**S&P 500 in real terms** 2.5
1954–2005

■ Log S&P500 Price Index adjusted for inflation using CPI dat
■ Log S&P500 Price Index adjusted for inflation and detrended using displaced moving average
○ Cycletops

Source: Thomson Financial

Table 2.1 **Dow Jones Industrial Average closing levels, 1904–2005**

|  |  |  |  | % change |
|---|---|---|---|---|
| Dec 31st 1904 | 69.61 | Dec 31st 1905 | 96.20 | 38.2 |
| Dec 31st 1914 | 54.58 | Dec 31st 1915 | 99.15 | 81.7 |
| Dec 31st 1924 | 120.51 | Dec 31st 1925 | 156.66 | 30.0 |
| Dec 31st 1934 | 93.36 | Dec 31st 1935 | 144.13 | 54.4 |
| Dec 31st 1944 | 152.32 | Dec 31st 1945 | 192.91 | 26.6 |
| Dec 31st 1954 | 404.39 | Dec 31st 1955 | 488.40 | 20.8 |
| Dec 31st 1964 | 874.13 | Dec 31st 1965 | 969.26 | 10.9 |
| Dec 31st 1974 | 616.24 | Dec 31st 1975 | 852.41 | 38.3 |
| Dec 31st 1984 | 1,211.00 | Dec 31st 1985 | 1,546.00 | 27.7 |
| Dec 31st 1994 | 3,833.00 | Dec 31st 1995 | 5,117.10 | 33.5 |
| Dec 31st 2004 | 10,783.01 | Dec 31st 2005 | 10,717.50 | −0.6 |
| Average |  |  |  | 32.9 |

## Interaction between the four-year and ten-year cycles

One of the most powerful influences on the four-year cycle is Juglar's ten-year economic rhythm. Four-year and ten-year cycles do not fit well together, being perfectly in step with each other only every 20 years. Consequently, as the two cycles interact with each other, a complex shape develops giving a different pattern from one decade to the next. The whole pattern repeats itself on a 20-year basis. The ten-year rhythm can also be skewed either positively or negatively by the longer-term secular trend.

The mid-point of the cycle is usually positive for the market. As Table 2.1 shows, since 1904 years ending in a five have seen an average gain of 32.9% in the Dow Jones Industrial Average Index. The only mid-decade year in which the Dow Jones index ended down was 2005.

### Elliott wave

In practice, the market ratchets either up or down in a series of two steps forward, one step back moves or, during downtrends, one step forward, two steps back.

As a result of his analysis of stockmarket data in the 1930s, Ralph Nelson Elliott discovered that this ratcheting process takes the form of a series of waves. He noticed that bull markets usually have a regular shape of three upward legs separated by two corrections. Bear markets also have a regular pattern: a fall, a rally and a fall. The falls usually alternate between sharp corrections and broader consolidations, during which the price eases lower. Each wave is made up of sub-waves that follow the same pattern, and this, in turn, can be broken down again. Elliott used nine degrees of waves.

There are some people today who attempt to fit every market move into an Elliott wave pattern and, with the benefit of hindsight, usually succeed. In practice, at its most detailed level, Elliott's work is not easy to apply to day-to-day decision-making, although the primary and secondary waves can be helpful in giving shape to the big picture.

### Psychology behind Elliott wave patterns

Markets ratchet up and down because the perception of most investors as to where the market is going is heavily influenced by where it has just been. They do not, therefore, benefit from a sense of perspective.

Figure 2.6 illustrates the point. Imagine an investor thinking in a series of time frames, and it is the last two time periods that appear to be the most relevant. At time period 1, the average investor sees that the market fell in each of the last two time frames and therefore expects this trend to continue (although in practice this turns out to be the bottom of the market). However, a few "value" investors, attracted into the market by low prices, will have embarked on some cautious buying, triggering an upturn. In the next time frame (time period 2), the average

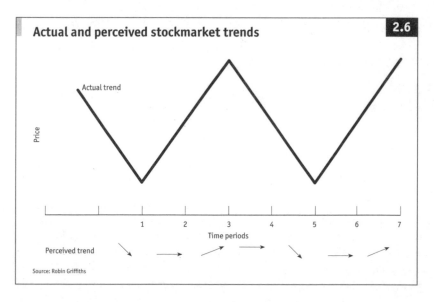

**Actual and perceived stockmarket trends**  2.6

Price

Actual trend

Time periods
1   2   3   4   5   6   7

Perceived trend

Source: Robin Griffiths

investor sees that the market rose in the most recent time frame but fell in the previous one and so perceives the market to be going sideways (although in practice it is on a rising trend). At the market top in the next time frame (time period 3), the general perception is that the market is rising because it rose in each of the two preceding periods. However, investors that got in at the bottom have decided to take their profits and start selling, so the market does not make any further upward progress. At time period 4, the average investor perceives the trend to be flat because it was down in the previous time frame but up in the one before that. It is not until between time periods 4 and 5 that the market is perceived to be on a falling trend, which causes heavy selling.

Figure 2.6 shows that the perceived market moves are exactly the same as the actual ones, except they are time-shifted by one period.

This delayed response to market trends is influenced by the general pattern of investing in the market and gives a skewed shape to overall investment behaviour. Figure 2.7 shows the percentage of investors over the market cycle who are bullish, bearish or neutral and the extent to which they commit their funds. At the bottom of the cycle, when almost everyone is bearish, the few who do invest commit only a small proportion of their funds, but as the groundswell of bullish sentiment rises, so does the money coming into the market. At the top of the market there will be some profit-taking, but sentiment is overwhelmingly bullish and most institutions will shift to a more neutral stance and refrain from committing new funds to the market rather than sell existing holdings. As the market continues to fall, a greater proportion of investors sell increasing amounts of their holdings until a trough is reached. So instead of having a regular pattern of investment and disinvestment

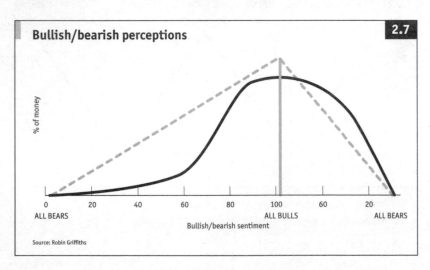

**Bullish/bearish perceptions**

2.7

% of money

0   20   40   60   80   100   60   20
ALL BEARS                    ALL BULLS        ALL BEARS

Bullish/bearish sentiment

Source: Robin Griffiths

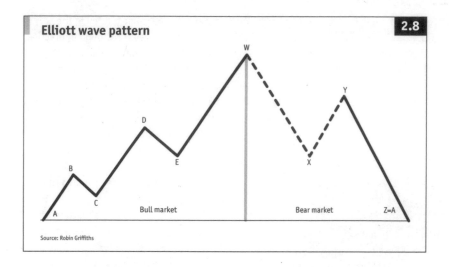

**Elliott wave pattern** 2.8

W

Y

D

E

X

B

C

Bull market

Bear market

Z=A

A

Source: Robin Griffiths

(which would give rise to a sine wave), the market moves in a skewed wave pattern as shown in Figure 2.7. This means that rather than being split into two equal halves of two years, the bullish phase of the four-year cycle usually lasts for 30 months and the bearish phase for 18 months.

If Figures 2.6 and 2.7 are combined, an Elliott wave pattern emerges (Figure 2.8). At the bottom of the cycle (A) investors generally perceive the market to be falling, but a few adventurous buyers go into the market, prompting a small rally. At point B these early buyers are ahead of the trend and take profits. The majority of investors still perceive the trend to be flat so they are not prepared to commit funds and there is a pullback to point C. This process is repeated again with a slightly larger number of buyers coming into the market, taking the rally to point D. The move from A to E occurs between time periods 1 and 2 in Figure 2.6. By the time point E is reached, both the perceived trend and the actual trend are up (time period 2 in Figure 2.6). Sentiment is in the 80–100% bullish range, giving rise to a strong impulsive rally up to W, which is the largest and longest leg of the bull phase.

At the top (point W), the same thing happens in reverse. The first selling signal tends to be muted. The fall-rally, shown as a dotted line on the first downward leg, is often difficult to distinguish and the rally phase may actually make a new high or at least form a double top pattern. The severe part of the fall occurs from Y to Z (between time periods 4 and 5 in Figure 2.6), the point at which both the perceived and actual trends are bearish.

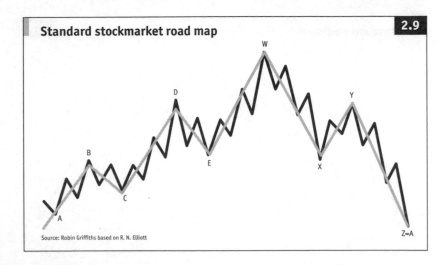

**Standard stockmarket road map** `2.9`

Source: Robin Griffiths based on R. N. Elliott

Figures 2.9–2.11 show how Elliott's ratcheting waves can be incorporated into the basic four-year cycle shown in Figures 2.1–2.4.

Where the longer-term trend is exerting a positive pull, the effect will be to distort the basic four-year cycle upwards, extending the upward waves and minimising the downward ones as shown in Figure 2.10.

Conversely, in a market experiencing a negative long-term trend, the reverse will occur. The downward moves will be extended and rallies will make relatively small progress, as seen in Figure 2.11.

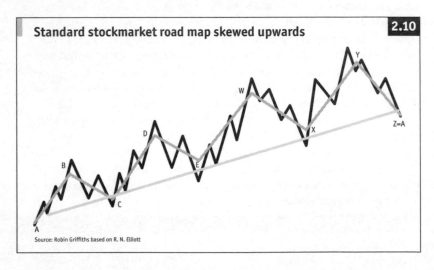

**Standard stockmarket road map skewed upwards** `2.10`

Source: Robin Griffiths based on R. N. Elliott

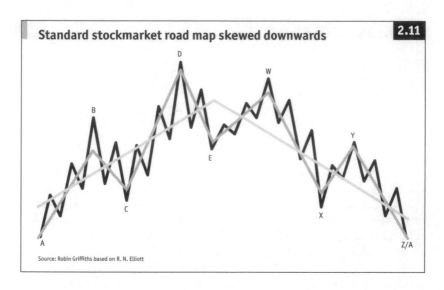

**Standard stockmarket road map skewed downwards** `2.11`

Source: Robin Griffiths based on R. N. Elliott

Essentially, all stockmarket indices are on one of the three road maps illustrated in Figures 2.9–2.11 and many of the markets have a strong positive correlation with each other. The four-year cycle overlaid with the appropriate longer-term trend gives investors a "road map" from which they can determine which countries or regions are likely to show outperformance against other markets.

# 3 Sector rotation

Cyclical analysis is useful in determining the correct asset weighting and global balance of a portfolio, but more detailed "mapping" techniques are needed to navigate the processes of sector allocation and stock selection.

Chapters 1 and 2 showed how cycles of bull and bear markets are driven by the cycles in the underlying economy, but with a time lag. The market discounts anticipated changes, not what is actually happening at present (unless it is some "external" event, such as a terrorist attack, which has not already been factored in, in which case the market quickly readjusts to accommodate this new information).

In the United States, the four-year cycle is closely connected to the political or electoral cycle. In trying to get re-elected, presidents cannot resist the temptation of tinkering with the economy in order to try and maximise the "feel-good" factor. This feeds through to interest rates and, consequently, sector rotation is largely interest-rate driven.

## The low point

At the low point or bottom of the stockmarket cycle, the economy is in a poor state and is expected to get worse. This gives rise to a view that interest rates will have to fall to counteract the economic downturn and, on the back of this expectation, interest-rate stocks start to perform well. At this stage in the cycle, banks generally take the lead, followed by other financial players.

As it becomes obvious that the economy is starting to recover, the bull trend in the stockmarket gathers momentum. The dominant force is now consumption. Stocks that move coincidently with the economy start to be the market leaders. High-street retailers, for example, feature regularly in stockmarket reports.

Financial stocks will not have peaked at this stage but, because they have been rising for longer relative to other sectors of the market, they do not seem so attractive and their rate of rise slows down. It is an axiom of technical analysis that relative strength (that is, a share's performance relative to the market as whole) will peak before the share price peaks. There are, therefore, more stocks rising than there were at the start of the bull phase and indicators aimed at gauging the breadth of market activity start to improve significantly. For example, the ratio of stocks showing a gain against those showing a decline starts to pick up significantly and the number of stocks trading above their rising moving average line also increases.

### The mid-point

In the middle of a bull run there is an across-the-board improvement in market sentiment and, whereas at the start of the cycle buying was largely confined to institutions, it now begins to spread out to the general public.

### Rising confidence

The next phase of the rally is driven by "the thundering herd". Not only are more people buying but they are more aggressive about how much of their funds they will commit to the stockmarket. Small market capitalisation growth stocks – and, indeed, stock tips generally – have a seductive sway. The level of valuations rises and extreme price/earnings ratios are justified on increasingly tenuous grounds. This is the phase of the cycle when irrational exuberance may set in and bubbles can occur. It is a time of great confidence and excessive optimism. Cassandra-like voices are drowned by promises of "a goldilocks economy", "the perfect paradigm" and, most treacherous of all, "it is different this time". This stage of the rally can carry on for a long time. Investors who have heard it all before take their profits too early and then spend frustrating months, even years, watching their opportunity costs rack up. The gains made through these impulsive moves can be substantial, so it pays to go with the flow but to be ruthless about closing out positions on any setback. The investment themes at this stage of the cycle tend to be small, expensive companies that have a compelling "story".

### The "impulsive" phase

During the "impulsive" phase of the uptrend, there comes a time when valuations are recognised as having gone too high and the economy begins to overheat. There is a tendency to concentrate less on earnings growth and more on asset value. Executives recognise that their company's equity is expensive and there is a rush of takeover activity. The commercial and domestic property sectors generally do well at this stage in the cycle.

It is also at this point that the sector laggards start to catch up. These are usually classic cyclical businesses, and as their share prices have not moved up as much as the early leaders they seem cheap by comparison.

Metals, minerals and resources normally trend positively at this time but their ratings never get to the glamorous levels that the small-growth sectors can attract. For many years, these commodities were in secular downtrend so tended to lag a long way behind faster-moving sectors. Driven by demand from China and other developing countries, commodities are now in a secular uptrend so will slowly acquire a more forward-looking valuation basis, but their place in the cycle will remain. This is already happening, for example with firms such as BHP Billiton.

## After the peak

Finally, the economy will be seen to have peaked and the optimists will be expecting a gradual slowdown and the pessimists will be anticipating a full-blown recession. The financial sector is the first to decline, but the malaise quickly spreads throughout the market. The indicators that monitor the breadth of market activity go into reverse although the market may still be rising, lulling the majority of investors into believing (and acting) as though the bull trend is still firmly in place. Some investors will, however, start increasing the bond weighting in their portfolios. Gradually, more investors will adopt a defensive strategy. The classic defensive sectors are tobacco, beverages, pharmaceuticals and utilities. They tend to pay good dividends, in some cases rivalling the return available on bonds. Psychologically, there is not only a reluctance to acknowledge the change in trend, but also a tendency to deny that it is occurring. For this reason some wild "special situation" stocks can perform well at this time and earlier bull themes may also catch a second wind. It is in fact their last gasp. Eventually the capitulation phase clicks in and the market declines to the bottom of the next cycle.

# 4 Stock selection

When it comes to choosing individual stocks, a "technical" reading of the share price is an effective way of identifying companies with upside potential, but you should not ignore the fundamentals of a company completely.

Technical analysis acts as a radar screen, picking up on the forces of supply and demand for any particular share or market. In this respect it is different from fundamental analysis. Fundamental analysts will try to put an intrinsic value on a company's share price. Although they may be correct in their analysis that a share's price is below its intrinsic value, they may have to wait years until the market comes round to their view. Unfortunately, patience is not one of the defining characteristics of the modern investment world. Fund managers and even pension-fund managers are measured on a quarterly basis. There are some investors who are still happy to play a long game, but in today's market most participants have short time horizons and are not prepared to wait for an investment acorn to grow into a flourishing oak.

Technical analysis also provides a rigorous money management system, since it injects an element of discipline into the critical timing decision of when to take a profit or cut a loss. Once a stock has been selected, there are automatic triggers that force analysts to review their original buy recommendation should the share price start falling rather than rising as anticipated. By contrast, if a fundamental analyst calculates that a share represents good value at a certain price and the price then falls by 10% without there being any change in the company's fundamentals, it will represent even better value at this lower level. "Better buying opportunities" – the euphemism used by stockbrokers when encouraging their clients to buy a company whose share price has fallen since their original recommendation – results in investors buying into a falling market.

By seeking to buy companies whose share prices are on an upward trend, technical analysis is trying to encapsulate Schumpeter's theory of "creative destruction" since companies in the new sectors of the economy will inevitably be growth stocks. By contrast, "value" investors could find themselves chasing stocks in dying sectors of the economy or buying companies whose efforts to reposition themselves at the more dynamic

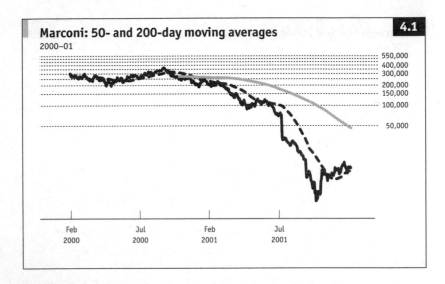

**Marconi: 50- and 200-day moving averages**
2000–01

4.1

550,000
400,000
300,000
200,000
150,000
100,000

50,000

| Feb | Jul | Feb | Jul |
| 2000 | 2000 | 2001 | 2001 |

frontiers of the economy have not been successful. Marconi, which started life as GEC, is a good example of the latter.

In the 1980s and the first half of the 1990s, under the aegis of Lord Weinstock, GEC was an extremely well-run holding company for a diverse range of "old economy" industrial businesses. It had built up a large cash reserve and there was some criticism that this had not been used to invest in new businesses. In 1996, when Lord Weinstock retired, the new management embarked on a policy of acquiring "new technology" companies with the object of shifting GEC's focus to the cutting edge of the economy – communications and information technology. When the defence business was sold to British Aerospace (now known as BAE Systems) in 1999, the company's transformation was marked by changing its name to Marconi (yet another example of how a name change can signal the start of corporate decline). In December 2001, some fundamental analysts put out a buy recommendation for Marconi. At the time this did not seem an outlandish idea (see Figure 4.1). A lot of the dotcom froth had been blown off the market and Marconi's share price was almost back to the level it had been in 1999 before the bubble had started inflating prices at an unsustainable rate.

Figure 4.2 shows what subsequently happened to the share price. It is possible that technical analysts might have incorrectly identified the share price's break up above the short-term moving average in December 2001 as a turning point and put out a buy recommendation. However, the

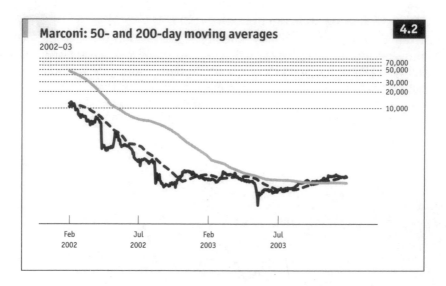

**Marconi: 50- and 200-day moving averages**
2002–03

70,000
50,000
30,000
20,000
10,000

| Feb | Jul | Feb | Jul |
| 2002 | 2002 | 2003 | 2003 |

4.2

next month the fall back below the shorter-term moving average signalled a loss of momentum that would have forced them to review their buy recommendation.

By picking up on the flow of funds, technical analysis is, therefore, effective in fine-tuning the timing of when to buy (or close out) a holding.

### A fundamental double check

Once a share has been highlighted as a buy by a technical indicator, it is useful to screen the fundamentals to check there is intrinsic value in the company and that it is not just some ethereal business that will disappear off the technical radar screen just as quickly as it appeared. The collapse of the dotcom boom in 2000 is a salutary example of what can happen if investors buy stocks just because they are going up, regardless of whether the company has made any profits or is likely to do so in the foreseeable future.

### Applying technical analysis across different markets

The tools of technical analysis can be applied to any market – shares, indices, bonds, currencies or commodities – where the price is influenced by the forces of supply and demand. As the main thrust of this section of this book is, however, to show how the tools of technical analysis can be used to select individual stocks, most of the examples chosen are equities.

### The power of positive momentum

Positive momentum is therefore the key to successful stock selection for investors looking for capital growth. The easiest way to gauge momentum is by looking at the trend line. In a rising market, a line drawn under a succession of lows will give an upward-sloping trend line; and in a falling market, a line joining the highs will produce a downward-sloping trend line. In a sideways moving market, the trend line will be flat.

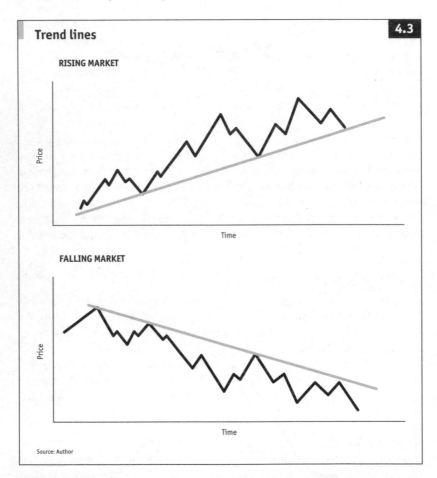

**Trend lines**  `4.3`

RISING MARKET

Price

Time

FALLING MARKET

Price

Time

Source: Author

### Trends within markets

Some academics scoff at the idea that markets move in trends and it is appropriate to comment on this debate at this point. These academics subscribe to the efficient market hypothesis, which argues that at any particular time all existing information is already priced into a market and so the next price movement will be independent of the previous one, indeed of any previous moves. The market, it is argued, takes a random walk (rather like a drunk in an open space) and so markets do not follow any patterns or trends. Any attempt to outperform the market is, therefore, pointless since it relies on luck rather than judgment.

In his book *The (Mis)Behaviour of Markets*, Benoit Mandlebrot, a mathematician, explains why this theory is flawed. A somewhat simplified version of his argument runs as follows. If markets were really random, price changes would be just as likely to be up as down and when many price changes were plotted on a chart they would fall into a normal or Gaussian distribution (forming the familiar bell-shaped curve shown as the continuous line in Figure 4.4). The characteristics of the standard bell curve are that variations of one standard deviation from the mean are common and occur 68% of the time; and 95% of all deviations will be within two standard deviations from the mean. So out of 100 price swings, moves as large as two standard deviations from the mean should occur on only five occasions. There is still a possibility of swings greater than this but they should in practice be rare. Mandelbrot studied the price movements of cotton (he focused on this market because he was able to obtain reliable records going back 100 years). What he found was that in

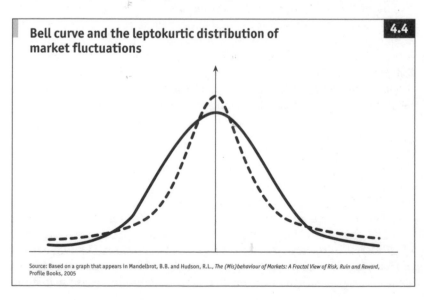

**Bell curve and the leptokurtic distribution of market fluctuations**

4.4

Source: Based on a graph that appears in Mandelbrot, B.B. and Hudson, R.L., *The (Mis)behaviour of Markets: A Fractal View of Risk, Ruin and Reward*, Profile Books, 2005

the real world price movements follow a leptokurtic distribution (shown as the dotted line in Figure 4.4). (A distribution is called leptokurtic – from the Greek word *lepto* meaning slim – if it is at the same time more peaked and with fatter tails than a normal distribution.)

Other markets have been found to behave in a similar way. Eugene Fama, a student of Mandlebrot's, studied 30 blue-chip stocks in the Dow Jones Index. He found that prices spend a long time making only small deviations; they seem to be range bound, clinging unnaturally to the mean. When they do move, the swings are substantial, with changes of seven or even ten standard deviations occurring. If price movements within a market conformed to the standard bell curve, a move of more than five standard deviations would occur only once every 7,000 years. But in practice what should be an incredibly rare fluke occurs with sufficient regularity to undermine the idea that market moves fit the standard bell curve.

According to Mandelbrot, there is considerable evidence to support the idea that prices exhibit "short-term dependence". In other words, a price change can be influenced by the behaviour of previous price changes. There is an internal momentum to the market. The authors believe that this internal momentum occurs because the markets are a function of human interaction and human crowds have a herd-like tendency. In the real world of the marketplace, it is this internal momentum that gives rise to trends that, as mentioned at the start of this book, appear more often and persist for longer than the laws of chance would allow. An essential skill for investors is, therefore, the identification of trends. However, Mandelbrot believes that future market moves can best be predicted by means of fractal geometry (a branch of science that he founded and that he defines thus: it "perceives the hidden order in the seemingly disordered, the plan in the unplanned, the regular pattern in the irregularity and roughness of nature").

### Relative strength

It is not sufficient to buy a share simply because its price is going up; in a rising market all shares will float up. In order to identify which shares have added zip and are rising faster than the market in general, it is helpful to look at their relative performance or strength. This involves measuring a sector or individual share price against that of a relevant index – for example, using the FTSE All Share index to assess the relative performance of UK shares or the S&P 500 for US equities. By plotting the relative trend of shares against the market, it is possible to make direct comparisons of shares within a particular sector. The relative trend of stocks against the

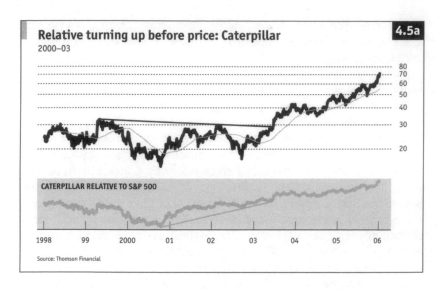

**Relative turning up before price: Caterpillar**
2000–03

`4.5a`

CATERPILLAR RELATIVE TO S&P 500

Source: Thomson Financial

market or against each other summarises the differences the market has drawn. It is also interesting how often a turning point will occur on the relative chart before it appears on the price chart (see Figures 4.5 and 4.6). Relative strength is, therefore, an extremely useful tool in the stock-picking process.

Relative strength can be quantified by calculating a share price or

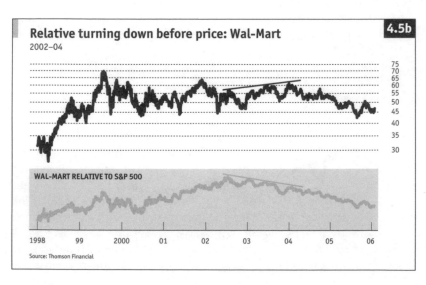

**Relative turning down before price: Wal-Mart**
2002–04

`4.5b`

WAL-MART RELATIVE TO S&P 500

Source: Thomson Financial

sector's rate of change over a period and comparing it with a) the relevant index and b) other shares. This enables companies' share price performance to be ranked.

### Moving averages

A moving average is a method of smoothing data over a chosen period of time and is useful in defining the trend of a market. There is no one magic period for a moving average. The period used should be proportionate to an investor's time horizon. The length of moving average that gives consistent support to a particular chart will vary a little but, in general terms, the price will move back to test the moving average in proportion to the length of the moving average used. Thus the 25-day moving average, for example, usually supports the fluctuations over a month fairly consistently, whereas it is normal for that of the 200-day moving average to be tested perhaps only once a year. A crossover of the price through a moving average often signals a change in trend.

The 200-day moving average establishes the direction of the primary trend of a market. A shorter moving average, such as the 25-day or 50-day, will pick up the secondary trend, which could be moving in the opposite direction. As Figure 4.6 shows, when a trend is established, the 200-day moving average trails quite a long way behind the price line and, as a result, it can sometimes be slow to signal a change in trend.

A short-term moving average is much more sensitive to trend changes

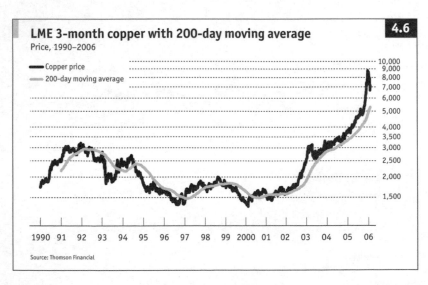

**LME 3-month copper with 200-day moving average**    `4.6`
Price, 1990–2006

— Copper price
— 200-day moving average

10,000
9,000
8,000
7,000
6,000
5,000
4,000
3,500
3,000
2,500
2,000
1,500

1990 91 92 93 94 95 96 97 98 99 2000 01 02 03 04 05 06

Source: Thomson Financial

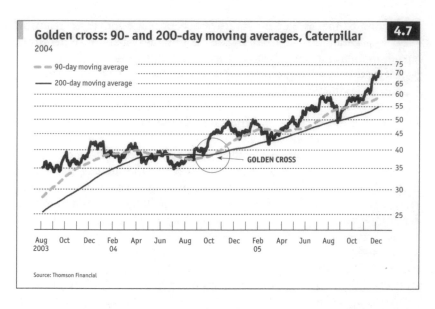

**Golden cross: 90- and 200-day moving averages, Caterpillar** `4.7`
2004

- - - 90-day moving average
——— 200-day moving average

GOLDEN CROSS

Aug   Oct   Dec   Feb   Apr   Jun   Aug   Oct   Dec   Feb   Apr   Jun   Aug   Oct   Dec
2003              04                                         05

Source: Thomson Financial

but is vulnerable to being "whipsawed" in and out of the market by short-term price volatility. Applying both a long-term and a short-term moving average helps to overcome some of the shortcomings involved in using a single average.

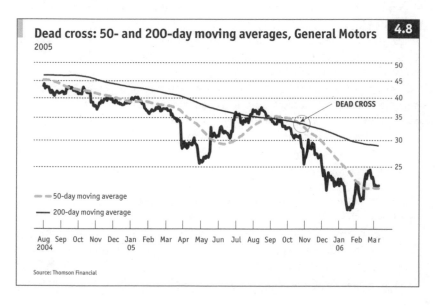

**Dead cross: 50- and 200-day moving averages, General Motors** `4.8`
2005

DEAD CROSS

- - - 50-day moving average
——— 200-day moving average

Aug Sep Oct Nov Dec Jan Feb Mar Apr May Jun Jul Aug Sep Oct Nov Dec Jan Feb Mar
2004              05                                              06

Source: Thomson Financial

39

A cross of the shorter moving average over the longer one can be used to generate buy and sell signals. If both averages are rising when the shorter-term average breaks above the longer one, it is known as a "golden cross" and suggests that bullish sentiment is growing stronger (Figure 4.7 on the previous page).

Conversely, a cross-over when both moving averages are falling is known as a "dead cross" and indicates an increasingly bearish outlook (Figure 4.8 on the previous page).

Moving averages can also be used to rank companies' momentum. By working out the percentage change per week of the moving averages, a rate of rise can be established. The basic premise is that the stronger the rise, the more attractive is the share, but this ranking can be qualified by other indicators.

### Overbought/oversold

Market or individual shares that are rising fastest are likely to become overbought. The point at which stocks become critically overbought (or oversold in a falling market) will vary according to the sector and general market conditions.

It is not advisable to use the extent to which a share is overbought as the sole reason to sell out of a stock or position completely, but it may be a useful trigger for crystallising a percentage of profits.

There are two ways of measuring the extent to which the market is overbought or oversold. One is the deviation above or below the long-term moving average. Fluctuations up to 20% above and below the 200-day moving average are normal, but most strong trends are likely to consolidate at least by the time the deviation reaches 30%. There will be exceptions to these thresholds but they give a useful measure of risk and highlight stocks or markets that need to be watched closely for signs of a major consolidation. Unwinding an overbought or oversold situation can take the price back to the 200-day moving average.

The RSI index developed by Welles Wilder, an American analyst, is another indicator that gauges the extent to which a market is overbought or oversold. (RSI stands for Relative Strength Index and should not be confused with relative strength compared to an index mentioned on page 36.) It is derived by calculating the average price rise during up days over a period of time (usually 14 days) divided by the average price fall during down days. The index ranges between 0 and 100. A reading of 70 or above suggests a market is moving into overbought territory, and a level of 30 or less implies it is becoming oversold. It must be stressed that these

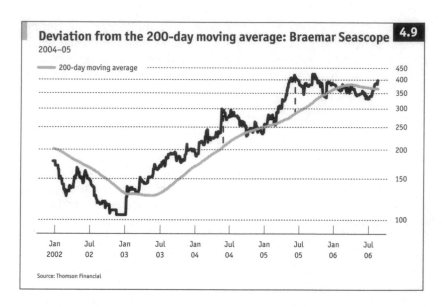

**Deviation from the 200-day moving average: Braemar Seascope** `4.9`
2004–05

━━━ 200-day moving average

Source: Thomson Financial

levels are not absolutes – shares frequently continue rising well above the 70 level or indeed falling below 30, and it is for this reason that over-bought/oversold indicators should be used only as a guide and not relied upon for firm buy and sell signals.

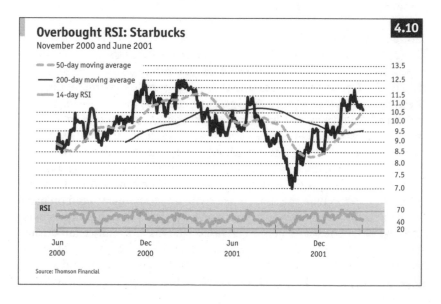

**Overbought RSI: Starbucks** `4.10`
November 2000 and June 2001

━ ━ 50-day moving average
━━━ 200-day moving average
━━━ 14-day RSI

RSI

Source: Thomson Financial

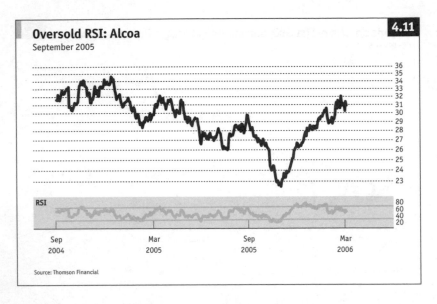

**Oversold RSI: Alcoa**
September 2005

4.11

Source: Thomson Financial

Some technical analysts find that divergences between the share price and the RSI provide a further level of fine-tuning that helps improve the reliability of this indicator. For example, a new high in the share price that is not confirmed by a new high on the RSI suggests that the upward momentum is slowing down.

### Support and resistance

One of the most useful and reliable features of technical analysis is high-lighting support and resistance levels. People tend to focus on certain price levels, either round numbers such as $1.70 or levels where the market has become trapped for some time. If a price is rising and consistently fails to push through a certain level, in technical terms, it is said to be encountering "resistance". Similarly, in a falling market, a level at which buyers repeatedly come in and start buying, thereby halting the downtrend, is known as "support". Ideally, these are the levels at which people aim to buy and sell. Support and resistance levels are determined by a variety of factors and, where these factors combine, clear areas of accumulation or dispersal emerge. Support and resistance levels are usually easy to identify, as can be seen in the share price of Tesco, a multinational retailer (Figure 4.12).

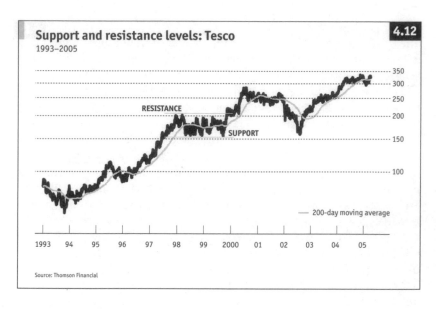

**Support and resistance levels: Tesco** `4.12`
1993–2005

RESISTANCE

SUPPORT

— 200-day moving average

1993  94  95  96  97  98  99  2000  01  02  03  04  05

Source: Thomson Financial

### Resistance turns to support

A level that has provided significant resistance during an uptrend is likely to become a support point in any subsequent retreat of the share price or market. Again, this is a result of the behavioural characteristics of the market crowd. When a share price that is on an uptrend encounters resistance, there will be a number of investors who are interested in buying but who have not, as yet, committed their funds. When the price finally pushes through the resistance level some of these investors will buy, but inevitably a number of potential participants will fail to do so. As the price continues to increase, they will be frustrated at missing out on a good buying opportunity and decide to buy these shares on the next price dip. When the price retreats down to the resistance level, this is the chance they have been waiting for and they start buying.

Conversely, in a downtrend, investors who bought at a support level begin to regret their investment as the price begins to fall steadily and they look for an opportunity to close out their position with as much of their investment intact as possible. So on any subsequent rally that takes the price back up to the support level at which they originally bought, they sell, and this level then acts as resistance, blocking further upward progress.

### New highs and lows

The break up to new levels in a rising market or down to new lows in a falling market can be significant because it often triggers fresh buying or selling momentum.

From the psychological perspective, the performance of the stockmarket is rather like that of an athlete who is trying to improve on his or her previous best time or distance. A new personal best generates a great buzz of excitement and positive feeling. Having achieved their goal, most athletes do not sit back and rest on their laurels but start looking ahead to the next challenge or objective. So it is with the markets. When a previous high is exceeded, investors start looking for the next target. When an athlete breaks a world record, it becomes front-page news. Similarly, when a market hits an all-time high, those usually completely uninterested in the financial markets suddenly take note and may even be tempted to start buying shares. Clearly uptrends do not go on forever. The positive impetus generated by reaching successively higher highs gradually begins to fade in a stale bull market. Instead, investors become more cautious and start booking profits until, eventually, the market rolls over – just as the mature athlete, eventually, has to retire.

There is also a technical reason why a move through a previous high indicates strong buying momentum. At market peaks there is usually an increase in trading activity as some investors take their profits while others buy into the market for the first time. As soon as the price begins to fall, disciplined investors will cut their position, but the evidence suggests that most investors are not disciplined. They persuade themselves that what might have been intended as a short-term punt is really a long-term investment. When the share price eventually creeps back towards the peak at which they bought, these "stale bulls" are anxious to close out what has been an unprofitable investment as quickly as possible. On the approach to a previous high, volume often rises as stale bulls rush to sell their holdings. So in order to push through the selling pressure generated by stale bulls, an uptrend must have considerable buying momentum behind it.

For example, an investor who bought Reckitt Benckiser at 1,300 pence in 1998 would have had the dismal experience of watching the share price lose more than half its value over the subsequent two years (see Figure 4.13). It was not until 2002 that the share price rallied back to its 1998 level and on three occasions it failed to break the 1,300 pence barrier. The break above 1,300 pence in 2003 triggered strong buying momentum.

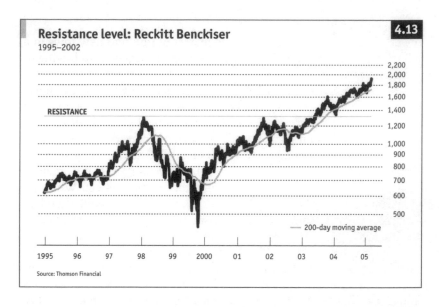

**Resistance level: Reckitt Benckiser**
1995–2002

`4.13`

RESISTANCE

2,200
2,000
1,800
1,600
1,400
1,200
1,000
900
800
700
600
500

—— 200-day moving average

1995    96    97    98    99    2000    01    02    03    04    05

Source: Thomson Financial

## Quantum advance and retracement levels

The legacy of W.D. Gann, a trader, to investment theory is the subject of controversy even among technical analysts. However, there is one area of his work, percentage moves, that does seem to correlate well with the way the market behaves. Gann noted that the size of each market wave tended to conform to specific percentages. These percentage moves tie in with Elliott's wave theory. Within each major trend there will be downward corrections (Elliott sub-waves). These retracements often pull back half or one-third of the recent gain, which may itself have retraced a recognisable fraction of a larger, earlier fall.

The rationale for quantum moves is that markets are driven by human beings, who think in whole numbers and easy fractions. They tend to draw lines and act at these easily recognised boundaries. Most common are 25%, 50% and 100%. Investors will, for example, happily watch their shares going up until one day they realise they have doubled in value, at which point they will decide to take some profits.

On any chart, half of the all-time high is always an important level. A move to a lower level tends to keep the stock depressed for a considerable period. If the chart is of an index, a move below half the all-time high suggests that the market is in a secular downtrend and will develop along the appropriate road map (as described in Chapter 2).

In the 1987 crash and the 2000 bear market, a great number of stocks

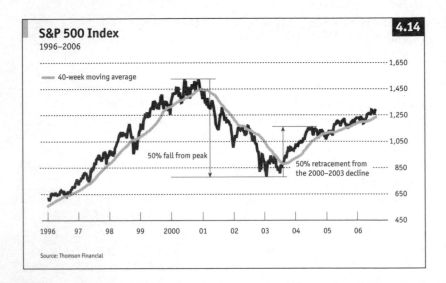

**S&P 500 Index**
1996–2006

`4.14`

— 40-week moving average

50% fall from peak

50% retracement from
the 2000–2003 decline

1,650
1,450
1,250
1,050
850
650
450

1996 97 98 99 2000 01 02 03 04 05 06

Source: Thomson Financial

fell by exactly half. After these falls, subsequent recovery rallies encountered resistance with surprising consistency at levels of 50% and 100% up from their low points.

Moves of one-third and two-thirds are also seen. Rather than one-third and two-thirds, some analysts use Fibonacci's levels of 61.8% and 38.2% (see box).

## Fibonacci ratios

Fibonacci was the *nom de plume* of Leonardo Pisano, a 13th-century Italian mathematician. In 1202 he wrote *Liber Abaci* (Book of Calculations), and one of the problems he investigated was how many rabbits would be produced in a year if you started off with a single pair. Certain parameters were set, such as each pair would always produce a pair, but essentially the sequence develops as follows:

1,1,2,3,5,8,13,21,34,55,89,144

Two interesting relationships emerge from this sequence:

☑ After the second term, each number is the sum of the two preceding numbers, for example 3 = 2+1, 5 = 3+2.
☑ When a number is divided by its preceding number, the ratio approximates to

1.618 (the further down the series you go, the closer the number is to 1.618). If a number is divided by the next number the ratio approximates to the reciprocal of 1.618, that is 0.618.

These are sometimes referred to as the "golden ratios". When applied to geometry, they can be used to produce a logarithmic spiral that begins and ends in infinity. The golden spiral occurs frequently in the natural sciences. The way the branches of a tree grow around the trunk and the pattern on a snail's shell, for example, both conform to the Fibonacci spiral pattern. (For further information about the Fibonacci sequence and its application in nature see Tony Plummer's book *Forecasting the Financial Markets*.)

The relevance of these ratios to the investor is that financial markets are driven by human beings who, without thinking about it, identify very readily with these natural golden ratios. The ratios are not infallible, but it is interesting how often the market will pull up after achieving these Fibonacci ratios. For example, in October 2005 the FTSE 100 index hit the 5,500 level, which represented a 61.8% retracement of the whole of the bear move from 1999 to 2003. Profit-taking immediately set in and it was not until almost three months later that the market pushed convincingly through this level.

These percentage moves are, of course, not infallible but they are consistent enough for investors to treat quantum moves of 38.2%, 50%, 61.8% and 100% with circumspection, especially if they coincide with other known support or resistance factors.

### Volume

The volume of trading activity in a market provides a useful guide to how much significance can be attached to a buy or sell signal. Any signal on a chart is much stronger for having been triggered by high volume. Rising volume in a trending market (a market that is moving either upwards or downwards, not going sideways) suggests that the bullish or bearish sentiment is being backed by the active participation of a growing number of investors. A new high that occurs against low or falling volume suggests the buying momentum behind the uptrend is on the wane.

The trend in trading activity is slightly different in a rising market than in a falling market. In a rising market, volume tends to build up gradually as more and more people start investing in the market until the trend becomes unsustainable and there is a blow-off at the peak, after

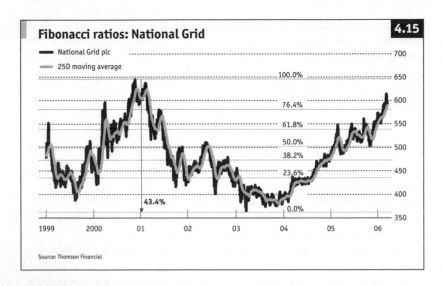

**Fibonacci ratios: National Grid**   `4.15`

— National Grid plc
— 25D moving average

100.0% — 700
— 650
76.4%
61.8% — 550
50.0%
38.2% — 500
23.6% — 450
— 400
43.4%
0.0% — 350

1999   2000   01   02   03   04   05   06

Source: Thomson Financial

which trading declines sharply. A falling market (especially in individual equities) does not attract the same rising volume until the rate of decline starts accelerating, at which point selling momentum tends to pick up. The final capitulation phase of a bear market is usually then characterised by a sharp increase in trading activity as investors lose their nerve.

The volume of trading activity alone should not be relied upon to give firm buy or sell signals, but it should be treated as a confirming indicator, particularly in respect of chart patterns.

## Chart patterns

To the uninformed observer, pattern analysis – with its sometimes curious terminology (head and shoulders, double bottoms) – might seem to be the point at which technical analysis becomes rather flaky. However, these patterns are just a visual representation of the branch of psychology known as crowd behaviour. Furthermore, most chart patterns represent a section of Elliott's wave pattern (see Figure 2.8 on page 25).

One of the basic tenets of technical analysis is that history repeats itself. In most other walks of life this is not a contentious statement, but it is treated with scepticism by some observers when applied to the financial markets. The reason technical analysts believe that history repeats itself is that markets are driven by humans who tend to react in a similar way to a given set of circumstances. The "self-love" that Adam Smith identified as the driving force of the market system is very much in evidence in the financial markets. Pulling in the opposite direction is the individual's fear of losing money. Aggregated to the crowd level, these two forces underpin bullish and bearish sentiment; and it is the battle between the bulls and bears that determines price. As in a military battle, there are conventional strategies that can be employed by both sides, although there are occasions when the battle does not proceed along one of these set-piece patterns of engagement. Chart analysis merely picks up on when the tussle between the bulls and bears is following a well-recognised course of action.

When a market pauses during an upward or downward trend, there is inevitably debate about whether it is just pausing to catch its breath or whether this is a more serious loss of momentum that harbingers a trend reversal. The pattern of the chart can sometimes provide a useful pointer as to what the next move is likely to be.

Chart patterns fall into two broad categories: those that signal a major reversal to the previously-established trend and those that a signal a continuation of the trend. The following examples are not an exhaustive list of the patterns in each category; they are merely intended to illustrate how the underlying ebbs and flows in buying and selling momentum are reflected on the charts.

### Reversal patterns

A trend rarely comes to an abrupt halt and then moves sharply off in the opposite direction. A change of trend is usually characterised by a period of uncertainty, as the buying or selling momentum begins to peter out and contrarian investors cautiously begin to commit funds in the opposite direction. (A contrarian investor is one who deliberately seeks to go against the prevailing market trend.) This hesitancy is reflected in the charts by a number of different patterns. With many of these patterns there is a key level (usually referred to as the "neckline") which, if broken, will signal that the contrarian investors have won the tug-of-war between the bulls and bears and that a major trend reversal is under way. If the price crosses back across this demarcation line, the signal given by the chart pattern is invalid.

Reversal patterns are most effective when they signal a change in direction of the primary trend; they do not, therefore, occur frequently. The most reliable patterns often take months or even years to develop.

**Head and shoulders.** Perhaps the best known reversal pattern is the head and shoulders, so called because it appears to trace out a human head and

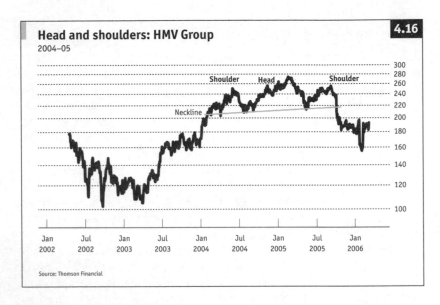

**Head and shoulders: HMV Group**
2004–05

`4.16`

Source: Thomson Financial

shoulders in silhouette. More importantly, it shows a market tracing out the middle section of Elliott's wave sequence.

The left-hand "shoulder" of the pattern develops when a steady uptrend that has been in place for some time falters. The price pulls back to a level where good support is found and investors who have missed out on the rise so far decide to take advantage of the price dip. This buying momentum drives the price up to a new high (shown as point W in Figure 2.9 on page 26). Profit-taking sets in and buyers again take advantage of the price dip, but this time the rally fails to reach the previous peak and the selling momentum is such that it cuts decisively through the neckline support level. The initial price target on the downside is the distance from the neckline to the peak of the "head" (see Figure 4.16). The pattern is negated if the price crosses up through the neckline again.

The volume of trading should fall while the head and second shoulder are being traced out and then rise sharply when the neckline is broken. Although this does not always happen, greater weight can be attached to the pattern if it is accompanied by falling volume, particularly when the second shoulder is being formed.

In a bear market, an inverse head-and-shoulders pattern signals a market bottom, with the height of the "head" giving the price target on the upside (see Figure 4.17).

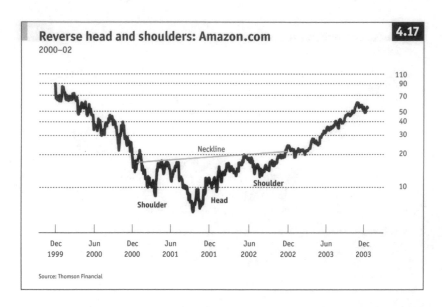

**Reverse head and shoulders: Amazon.com**
2000–02

*Labels: Neckline, Shoulder, Shoulder, Head*

Source: Thomson Financial

4.17

**Double tops and bottoms.** A double top is a slightly shortened version of the head-and-shoulders pattern. After reaching a peak, the price falls back to the support level. Buyers step in at this point and drive the price higher again, but the rally fails to push above the previous peak and profit-

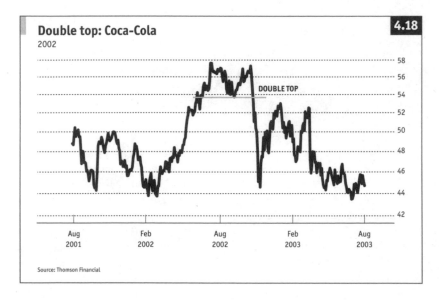

**Double top: Coca-Cola**
2002

*Label: DOUBLE TOP*

Source: Thomson Financial

4.18

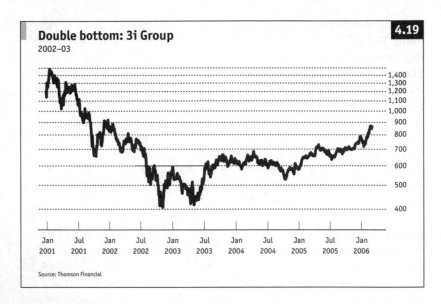

**4.19**

**Double bottom: 3i Group**
2002–03

Source: Thomson Financial

taking sets in, taking the price below the previous support level. The price objective is projected by measuring the distance from the neckline to the peak. Volume should be lighter on the right-hand shoulder but rise when the price falls below the neckline.

**4.20**

**Triple top: AstraZeneca**
2000–02

Source: Thomson Financial

A mirror image of the double top often marks the low point of a bear trend. The psychology of a double bottom is similar to that of a double top. Investors tentatively buy at the low and take profits after a short rally. The resulting sell-off takes the price back down to the low, where much more aggressive buying pushes the price above the neckline. With this pattern, the volume of trading should increase on the second rally.

**Triple tops.** This is a variation of the head and shoulders, but it does not occur nearly so often. Essentially, the head and both shoulders peak at the same level. Again an inverse triple bottom signals the reversal of a downtrend. Volume usually diminishes on each successive run up to a peak.

**Rounded bases or tops.** This is the one reversal pattern that does not have a clear demarcation line signalling when contrarian investors are in the ascendancy. Buying or selling momentum begins to fade as investors who have been chasing the trend feel the price has gone far enough but contrarian investors are not yet sufficiently confident to commit funds to the market in the opposite direction. The chart, therefore, traces a rounded top or bottom (sometimes referred to as a saucer), reflecting a much more gradual change in sentiment (see Figure 4.21).

**Rounded base: Great Portland Estates** 4.21
2002–04

Source: Thomson Financial

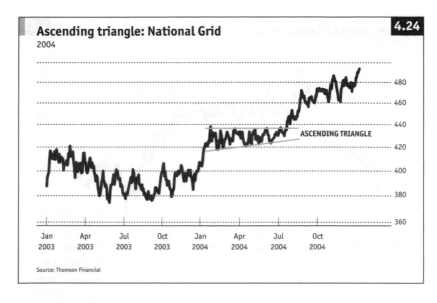

**Ascending triangle: National Grid** `4.24`
2004

Source: Thomson Financial

after the sharp move looks like a flag on top of a long flagpole (hence the name). These are short-term patterns and the maximum duration for the consolidation is a few weeks. If the flag lasts for more than four weeks, there is unlikely to be another strong impulsive move as this pattern generally occurs in fast-moving markets. The second rally or decline usually extends the same distance as the first impulsive move (see Figure 4.27 on page 58).

## Choosing which indicator to use

Like a general mulling over various military strategies in the light of the terrain and prevailing conditions, when it comes to deciding which technical tools to apply to a market at any particular time, an investor needs to evaluate the background conditions. For example, in a market that is in the grip of a buying frenzy, resistance levels may not carry much significance; whereas in a period of flat trading when volumes are low, they may act as concrete barriers, effectively blocking further upward progress.

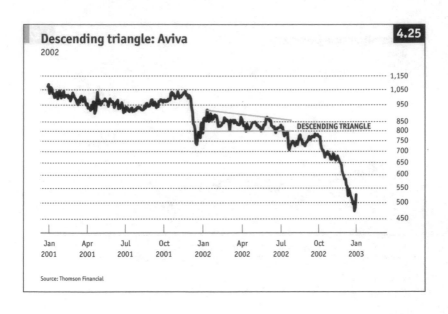

**Descending triangle: Aviva**
2002

`4.25`

DESCENDING TRIANGLE

Source: Thomson Financial

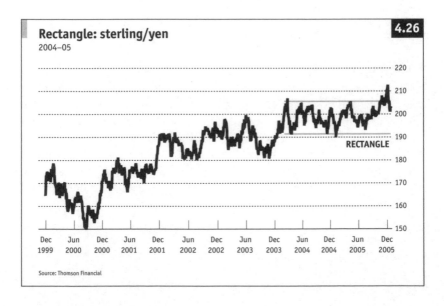

**Rectangle: sterling/yen**
2004–05

`4.26`

RECTANGLE

Source: Thomson Financial

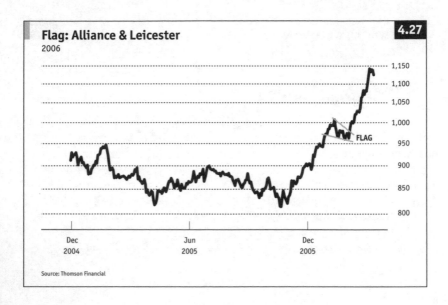

**Flag: Alliance & Leicester**
2006

4.27

Source: Thomson Financial

# PART 2
# LONG-TERM CYCLICAL DRIVERS

Over the course of history the most powerful driver of long-term growth has been industrialisation. Many countries have either undergone this economic rite of passage or are in the process of doing so. Countries that are in the early stages of this economic transition include China, India, Brazil and Russia. As these huge economies catch up with the G7 group of industrialised economies, they are likely to give a strong upward boost to global growth. Chapter 5 gives a brief overview of the great potential of the two largest "catch-up" countries, China and India, as well as some of the pitfalls they face.

Demographic patterns also have a strong impact on long-term economic growth. The relative demographic patterns in the United States, Asia and Europe are examined in Chapter 6.

Innovation is the third force responsible for driving the upward phase of the long-term economic cycle. A number of industries appear to be on the cusp of a new wave of innovation and are likely to give an upward impetus to global economic growth over the coming decades. Chapters 7 and 8 examine two areas – energy and biotechnology – where the scale of change is such that it is likely to affect the secular trend.

A number of the economic themes that are likely to have a significant effect on global growth are interconnected. For example, the raw materials needed to effect the catch-up process in developing countries will inevitably increase competition for the world's finite supply of natural resources. The most visible example of this has been the sharp rise in the oil price (see Figure P2.1 on the next page). Initially, the increased demand for raw materials is bound to cause friction as countries scramble to secure sufficient supplies for their own domestic consumption. But, looking further ahead, high prices will spur the search for alternative sources of energy.

The area of biological sciences is a classic example of how a new discovery can spark off a plethora of new innovations in related fields. Chapter 8 looks at how the decoding of the human genome in February 2000 started a "domino effect" of new technologies in medicine and information technology.

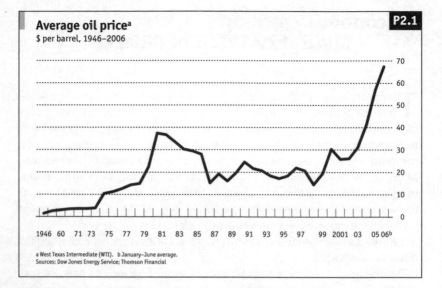

**Average oil price[a]**
$ per barrel, 1946–2006

P2.1

a West Texas Intermediate (WTI).  b January–June average.
Sources: Dow Jones Energy Service; Thomson Financial

# 5  Economic catch-up

The process of industrialisation, whereby a country gradually switches from depending primarily on agriculture to provide the main source of its wealth to manufactured goods and services, is the most powerful spur to economic growth. This was evident in Britain, France and Germany in the 1800s, in the United States a century later and in Japan in the 1980s. Many of the East Asian "tiger" economies are already well on their way to making this transition. But a number of large economies are still at an early stage of the process and it will be their industrialisation that will propel the long-term cycle upwards in future years.

China is the emerging economy that has received most attention, but there are some economists who believe that India will eventually prove to be an equally if not more important economic power. Latin America – and Brazil in particular – is still a long way from achieving its full economic potential while Russia – despite being rich in natural resources and having a huge land mass – lags a long way behind the rest of Europe in terms of gross domestic product (GDP) per head.

There are various ways of trying to measure the "catch-up" potential of these emerging countries, but one simple yardstick is to look at GDP per head.

Table 5.1 **GDP per head, 2005**

|            | $       |
|------------|---------|
| US         | 42,125  |
| UK         | 36,690  |
| Japan      | 35,824  |
| Russia     | 5,340   |
| Brazil     | 4,370   |
| China      | 1,700   |
| India      | 733     |
| G7 average | 37,670  |
| World      | 7,340   |

Sources: Economist Intelligence Unit; Thomson Financial

Catch-up potential is, therefore, defined here as the difference between a country's GDP per head and that of the equivalent measure for the average G7 industrialised countries. As can be seen from Table 5.1, there is currently a sizeable gap between countries such as China and India and the G7 average. As the industrialisation process gathers momentum, the gap will narrow and this catch-up growth will have a positive impact on longer-term economic trends.

It is not the purpose of this book to give a detailed analysis of the opportunities and potential pitfalls that face individual countries as they face up to the challenges of the technology revolution and globalisation, but an overview of the two largest, China and India, will demonstrate the significance of the next wave of industrialisation to the global economy.

## China

For years China has been regarded in economic terms as a slumbering giant. In the second half of the 20th century, Japan led an economic renaissance of East Asian countries such as South Korea and Singapore, but China was much slower to join in the process of economic awakening. Indeed, in November 2003 Erkki Liikanen, then European Commissioner for Enterprise and Information, noted that two years earlier "China was not on the map". China's admittance to the World Trade Organisation (WTO) in December 2001 was the catalyst for the country's recent explosive growth in international trade.

One of the reasons for the excitement about China's economic transition is the size of its potential market. At around 1.3 billion, the population of China is about five times that of the United States. Although China did not make much of an impact on the financial markets until the start of the 21st century, it has, nevertheless, been growing at an astonishing rate of 9.5% over the past two decades. Growth really began to take off in the 1980s when Deng Xiaoping started the process of "opening up" the country in 1983.

The official target is for gross domestic growth to quadruple in the two decades from 2001 to 2020, implying a compound growth rate of just over 7% a year. The Chinese authorities took the view that trying to sustain such a fast rate of growth in a centralised command economy would be logistically impossible, so it was decided that the economy would become more market-oriented. Reorienting an economic system is not easy, and the Chinese government decided that it would not relax political constraints until the economic revolution had yielded some tangible benefits (it is by no means certain that they will do so even then).

As well as moving away from a rigorous, centrally planned economic system, China is in the process of changing from a predominantly agrarian economy to an industrialised one. A major challenge will be the assimilation into the economy of the workers made redundant by the process of industrialisation. In 2004, the IMF estimated there were approximately 160m surplus workers in the rural economy and state-owned enterprises. The labour market will have to absorb not only these workers but also the new entrants. Many agricultural workers will migrate from the countryside to the towns as the rural economy becomes more industralised. It is this migration that will drive the secular uptrend in the medium term. At present there are considerable impediments to labour-market mobility because of the household registration system. Residency permits are used to allocate educational and governmental services, and it is hard for people to obtain these services if they move away from their officially-designated place of residence. However, the authorities have indicated that they are planning to ease some of these restrictions in order to reduce disguised unemployment in the rural areas. (Disguised or hidden unemployment occurs when workers do not achieve their maximum economic potential.) In the longer term, the negative demographics emanating from the "one child per family" policy and the skewed ratio of boys to girls will tilt the secular trend sharply downwards. But for the next decade, the positive effect of urbanisation is likely to outweigh the negative demographic trend.

### Economic problems
Such a dramatic transition is bound to be fraught with difficulties. One of the problematic areas is the banking sector. In the past, Communist Party committees have played an important role in the running of banks. Instead of basing investment decisions on commercial criteria, loans have been made to companies or individuals that satisfy an official checklist. Sectors or industries that the government wants to promote receive subsidised loans. The absence of a market to price capital results in it being allocated inefficiently. Furthermore, China's dynamic export-led growth means that there has been more money in the financial system than the banks can profitably invest, so there has been no rationing pressure to discriminate between good and bad investments.

The rudimentary state of the stockmarket and corporate bond market restricts the funding options available for companies wanting to raise capital. As a result, Chinese businesses rely largely on banks for their funding. In 2003, loans made by financial institutions amounted to

Rmb3 trillion (26% of GDP), compared with Rmb136 billion raised on the stockmarkets (1% of GDP) and Rmb36 billion (0.3% of GDP) by way of corporate bonds.

The government is taking steps to recapitalise the state banking system, and the opening up of China's banking and insurance markets in 2007 under the terms agreed with the WTO will add urgency to the reform process. But the banking system's lack of sophistication raises questions about its ability to underpin future economic development.

For a developing country, the level of domestic savings is unusually high. With only one child per family, people cannot rely on the next generation to look after them in their old age and the public pension system currently covers only 14% of the population. There has not, therefore, been a need for overseas funding to bolster domestic savings. However, attracted by the potential size of the market and government incentives, there has been a substantial inflow of overseas investment into the Chinese economy. In the early 1990s foreign direct investment (FDI) amounted to 6% of China's GDP and since 2000 it has fallen to 3.5%. More important than the capital itself has been enhanced productivity as a result of the management skills and technology that have been injected into the economy through FDI.

### Socialist stockmarket with Chinese characteristics

China's stockmarkets (based in Shanghai and Shenzhen) have to grapple with the inherent contradiction of equity ownership in a country that in the past has not recognised property rights. Companies whose sole objective previously was to meet the production quota laid down by some central government agency must now come to terms with the concept of maximising shareholder value. An added complication is the state's retention of a majority shareholding in listed companies. The pragmatic architects of China's "socialist market economy" have managed to thread their way through this philosophical challenge by developing an extremely intricate rule-based accounting system that is bolstered by an equally convoluted legal structure of share categories and corporate law. But change is in the air and the government has pledged to modernise and simplify the law relating to companies and bankruptcy.

The state's ownership of almost two-thirds of shares (by either central or regional government) casts an uncomfortable shadow over China's stockmarkets. Furthermore, the government's majority shareholding of non-tradable shares prevents the market forces of "creative destruction" from reallocating resources from inefficient companies to more productive ones. However, the government is looking at ways of moving these non-tradable shares into private hands. Having learnt from their experience in June 2001, when a State Council proposal that a proportion of future expenditure could be funded through the sale of state shares precipitated a collapse in the stockmarkets, the government will try to minimise the disruptive effects of this transition.

### Developing a more market-oriented environment

It is not just the stockmarket that is inadequate to deal with the demands of an economy the size of China's: the move to a more market-led economic environment must be bolstered by institutions and regulations which were not needed under the previous centrally controlled system but are essential to ensure the smooth running of any market.

Inefficient allocation of resources is creating bottlenecks in some areas of the economy and overcapacity in others. For example, a proliferation of nuclear power stations in the late 1990s led to a glut of power, but the excess capacity was then absorbed by the next wave of industrialisation so that companies again faced power rationing in the early 2000s. To meet the rising demand for energy, the authorities have commissioned more power plants, but a vice-minister of the National Development and Reform Commission has predicted that this is likely to result in considerable overcapacity in 2006 and 2007.

Although the economy has become more market-oriented, the transition has not gone as far as allowing private ownership of land. Farmers, for example, obtain 30-year leases from the state which can be rescinded without any right of appeal if the village committee approves the reallocation of the land for industrial use. The compulsory reappropriation of farming land around the edge of cities for development is provoking unrest, which sometimes escalates into serious riots.

The lack of a sophisticated independent legal system is a serious obstacle to economic development. International pressure to enforce intellectual property rights more rigorously will be difficult to achieve under the present local judicial system. But establishing an independent judicial system would mean creating an authority that could operate outside the constraints of the Communist Party.

Unemployment is another potential problem. It is currently estimated to be running at around 5%. According to the 2000 census, over 60% of the population still live in rural areas where there is a considerable amount of disguised unemployment. As agriculture becomes more efficient through greater mechanisation, unemployment will rise, spurring migration from rural areas to urban areas, which will have difficulty in assimilating a sudden rise in population numbers.

## Political problems

Apart from the economic problems that face a society in transition, China must also negotiate its way through a labyrinth of domestic and international political issues. China is not a democracy, and there is a potential contradiction in allowing greater economic liberalism while maintaining a political structure based on communism. People who have contributed to the country's economic boom may become increasingly resentful that they are not allowed any political participation. Migration from the countryside to the towns and cities will test the social fabric of the country to its limits. Protests against falling standards of living by rural workers and the pollution of rivers and wells – common grievances for a country undergoing industrialisation – are growing.

Externally, the long-standing problem of Taiwan and hostile relations with Japan occasionally prompt bouts of sabre-rattling by the Chinese government. If one of these episodes were to spill over into military conflict, it would obviously have adverse implications for China's drive to become a superpower. A more immediate threat is the friction that China's rise to become "the workshop of the world" has generated in other countries, particularly the United States. Although China's trade balance with the rest of the world was a net surplus of $25 billion in 2003, its trade surplus with the United States was $55 billion, and this is rising sharply. (China's relatively small overall surplus is achieved because it runs a large deficit with Japan and its other Asian trading partners.) The United States has already imposed trade quotas and tariffs on some Chinese imports, and as exports account for approximately 40% of the Chinese economy, any action that reined back this sector would cut overall growth sharply.

Energy is another area of potential conflict with the United States both directly and indirectly. The International Energy Agency predicts that by 2030 China will be importing around the same amount of oil as the United States: 10m barrels per day. To secure sufficient supply to meet this demand, China has been seeking to invest in foreign oil companies and to sign long-term contracts with producer countries. But in 2005 the China National Offshore Oil Corporation (CNOOC) was forced to withdraw its takeover bid for the US oil company Unocal in the face of political opposition from Congress. Building a strategic relationship with countries such as Iran, Sudan and Venezuela has also raised eyebrows in the United States. But in deference to China's support for the war on terror, the US authorities have, so far, merely registered quiet disapproval.

## India

India is the other giant economy that is in the throes of industrialisation, although it has lagged well behind China in terms of economic momentum. Over the past 20 years the Chinese economy has grown at an average rate of 9.5% a year while India has struggled to maintain a growth rate of 6%. Yet some economists believe that China and India's development will prove to be the economic equivalent of the race between the hare and the tortoise.

The fundamental difference between the two countries is that India is a democracy. There are not, therefore, the inherent contradictions of operating a market economy within a one-party political framework, but India's linguistic and religious divisions often result in weak coalition governments that lack the power to implement much-needed radical reforms. Federal politics adds another tier of inefficiency and corruption to the decision-making process.

India's other great advantage is proficiency in English – globalisation's *lingua franca* – among those who have received an education. However, education is far from universal, and in 2000, 35% of the population was illiterate (compared with just 9% in China).

### *Post-independence economic strategy*
After independence the Indian government was keen to throw off the yolk of colonialism, so, heavily influenced by the Soviet Union's economic model, the main focus of its economic policy was on import substitution. And, like the Soviet Union, a series of five-year plans was drawn up. Under the direction of this centralised planning system, the emphasis was on heavy and capital-intensive industry. To protect these nascent industries, high trade tariffs were erected. A private sector was allowed to develop, but it was hedged around with a complex web of controls and licences to ensure that investment flowed into the "right" sectors of the economy. To build up management capability, a decision was also taken to place all the emphasis in education on the tertiary sector. This economic strategy neither took advantage of India's strength – abundant labour – nor took into account its weakness – little capital – with the result that the country was condemned to years of relatively weak growth.

### The reasons for India's slow start

Some economic reforms were introduced in the late 1980s, but India's economic awakening really started in 1991 when Manmohan Singh, then finance minister and subsequently prime minister, announced a package of reforms which catapulted the economy out of the sluggish 4% growth rate that had prevailed for most of the post-war period into a more dynamic phase. The package included trade liberalisation, the removal of capital controls and industrial licensing and a general refocusing of economic policy to make it more market-oriented.

But the legacy of the earlier era remains. This is one of the reasons India has not followed the development pattern adopted by most other Asian countries of focusing on export-led manufacturing growth.

Trade tariffs remain high despite the reforms. At 22%, average tariffs are double those of other emerging Asian economies and have kept India a relatively closed economy. It has therefore not participated in the global economy to the same extent as China. India accounts for only 2.5% of world trade in goods and services, compared with China's 10.5%. The present government led by Manmohan Singh is committed to further liberalisation, and the IMF estimates that by 2009–10 exports will have more than doubled from their 2004–05 level and imports will have tripled.

Another factor that has hampered India's development is the country's woefully inadequate infrastructure. Bad roads, blocked ports and irregular supplies of electricity and water seriously handicap the transition to a more industrial economy. The scope for government-funded improvements to the infrastructure is limited by the size of the fiscal deficit, but the government is looking at public–private partnerships as a possible way of improving public services.

By focusing on the development of service industries, India has to some extent sidestepped the major obstacle of its infrastructure in improving its growth performance. Lack of an efficient transport network is not as much of a problem for businesses such as call centres, data processing and software development as it is for heavy industry. But these industries employ only a small proportion of the workforce, so if the huge pool of unemployed labour is to be tapped, a more labour-intensive manufacturing base will have to be developed. According to an IMF Working Paper, *India's Pattern of Development: What Happened, What Follows?*, rather than increasing its proportion of manufacturing industries, "India is actually veering further away from labour-intensive industries".

India's bureaucracy and red tape, particularly in relation to labour laws, have created an unfavourable investment environment. This is one of the reasons, according to Angus Maddison, author of *The World Economy: A Millennial Perspective*, that in 1998 FDI per head was just $14 in India compared with $183 in China; even in 2004 India received only one-tenth of the $60 billion FDI that China was given. But there are signs of a change in attitude on the part of both the Indian government and investors. The creation of special economic zones has encouraged companies such as Microsoft to increase their investment in the country, and inward invest-ment to India has been growing steadily in recent years.

The concentration on skill-intensive services has created a shortage of skilled labour. According to Mercer, a human resources consultancy, Indian salaries are rising at 12.8% against an inflation rate of 5.5%. The lack of skilled workers highlights the narrow education base. Although India has some excellent higher education institutions, in 2000 more than one-third of the population was still illiterate.

Whether the Indian tortoise will eventually catch up and even overtake the Chinese hare depends on two things:

- the extent to which the Indian government can tackle the domestic barriers to growth – inadequate infrastructure, bureaucratic red tape, import restrictions, low level of savings and restricted access to education;
- when the finishing line is drawn.

Demographic trends mean that, according to the UN population report, India's population will overtake China's by 2030, although the immediate challenge for the Indian government is to absorb the current available labour force into the productive economy.

## Economic catch-up is on an unstoppable path

For different reasons, the transition of China and India to industralised economies will not be smooth, but the process is now unstoppable. Their growth trajectories may at times resemble rollercoasters with some severe switchbacks along the way, but the underlying trend will, nevertheless, be upwards.

# 6 Demographic trends

The process of industrialisation prompts demographic changes within a society. Pre-industrial societies are characterised by high fertility and mortality rates, but as a country industrialises both of these tend to fall substantially.

Demographic shifts can have a powerful effect on economic growth. However, it is not the overall size of a population that influences growth but rather the age structure within a population. According to research carried out by the IMF, there is a positive correlation between a country's GDP growth per head and the size of its working-age population (15-64). Not only does a large, active labour force boost productive capacity, it also generates a high level of savings which stimulates investment, thereby enhancing output. Furthermore, there is a negative correlation between the number of elderly people (those aged 65 and over) in a population and the rate of growth of income per head.

In pre-industrial societies the majority of people are hunter-gatherers or farmers. Infant mortality is high. As recently as 150 years ago, life expectancy in the western world was only 45. Having a large number of children was in effect the "pension plan", and there is still an assumption that children will provide for their parents in old age in many poorer countries where it is normal for a healthy woman to have six or seven children and to lose some at birth or during childhood. In agrarian societies, if the birth rate is such that the country does not have enough food for its people, the ensuing famine brings population numbers down. As a result, up until the 20th century the world population grew very slowly. Industrialisation triggered the start of the growth in population numbers. But even then, the annual rate of growth of the world population remained at 0.5% between the 17th and 20th centuries. It was not until the second half of the 20th century that the rate began to accelerate sharply, reaching a peak of 2% in 1965-70. It has subsequently fallen back and is currently estimated to be 1.2% a year.

The traditional "snapshot" age structure of a society is that of a pyramid with a large, young population at the bottom. There is a gradual decrease in the population of higher age groups until at the top of the pyramid there is a small group of elderly people. However, as a result of significant changes in demographic trends, this pyramid shape is gradually changing and in some countries will invert. It is a global phenomenon, but different regions of the world are at different stages in the transition process. Japan and Europe, where population growth is almost zero, are at the forefront of this demographic change whereas the Middle East and some countries in Asia (such as India) still retain the traditional pyramid population structure.

## Demographic transition

At the bottom of the pyramid in countries where the transition is already well under way, fertility rates (the number of births per woman) have fallen sharply, causing population growth to slow and the proportion of young people relative to the population as a whole to fall. A fertility rate of 2.1 is needed to keep a population stable. In many parts of the developed world fertility rates have fallen well short of this level. Greater acceptance of birth control in countries such as Spain and Italy, for example, has meant that their fertility rates have fallen dramatically to 1.15 and 1.21 respectively. Even though fertility rates may recover slightly in these countries, the UN predicts that they are likely to remain below the replacement level in most developed countries over the next 50 years. With a fertility rate of 2.11, the United States is the only developed country where the fertility rate is equal to the replacement rate. Fertility rates in other parts of the world are much higher, but by 2050 the UN expects that in three out of four of the less-developed countries they will have fallen below the replacement rate. (Predicting future demographic trends is difficult. In 2003, the UN produced a detailed estimate of population trends to 2050. The biggest uncertainty surrounds fertility projections, so in addition to its central "medium" fertility scenario, the UN constructed "low" and "high" fertility scenarios. The figures quoted here are from the medium scenario.)

At the other end of the age pyramid, improved health care and living standards mean that more people are living longer. Not only is the proportion of elderly people growing, but their life expectancy is rising. The UN predicts that for the world as a whole, average life expectancy will rise from 65 years in 2002 to 74 years in 2045–2050, while the median age of the world population is expected to increase from 26.4 years in 2000 to 36.8 years in 2050 (this is the age that separates the global population into two halves). Again, there are huge disparities between different countries: in Japan life expectancy in 2002 was 81.6 years, and in Zambia it was only 32.4 years.

Globally, the number of elderly people is set to triple from 606m in 2000 to almost 1.9 billion in 2050. However, the "oldest-old" group

# Demographic trends in the US, France, China and India
2000, 2025 and 2050

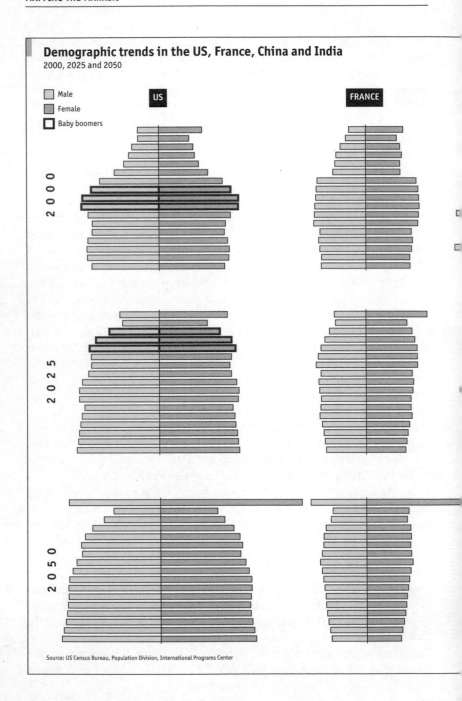

Source: US Census Bureau, Population Division, International Programs Center

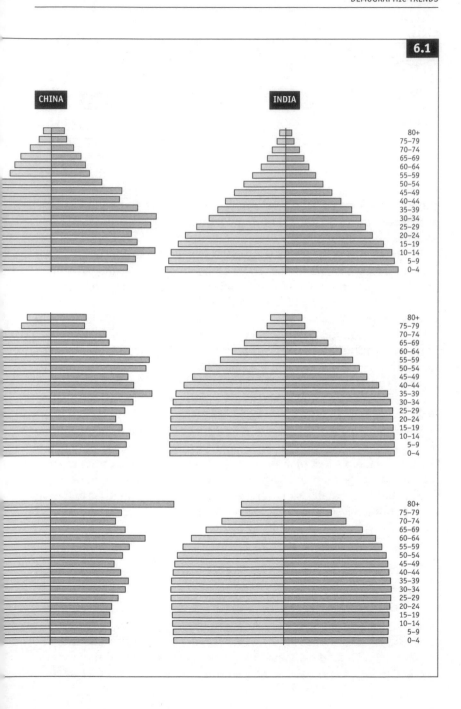

(80+ years) is expected to grow the fastest. In 2000 there were just 69m people aged 80 or older in the world, but by 2050 the number is expected to rise to 377m. In 2002 there were 50,364 centenarians in the United States, but it is estimated that 500,000 baby boomers will live to be 100 years old. In the UK, the Office for National Statistics forecasts that the number of people living to 80 years and beyond will double to almost 5m by the early 2050s. Yet by then the vast majority of this elderly cohort – 265m – will be living in less-developed countries.

As can be seen in Figure 6.1, India's demographic profile in 2000 was a perfect pyramid. There are far more young and middle-aged than old people. Those doing the work and paying taxes can easily afford the pensions of the old. This sort of demographic picture can support strong growth almost indefinitely.

In 25 years' time the top of the picture is still a pyramid, but the lower half has become parallel sided. There are too many old relative to young people, but the situation is still sustainable. Some economic growth is still possible but the compound rate will slow down.

In 50 years' time, even in India, the demographic picture will be fully mature. Although the diagram still tapers to the top, it is, nevertheless, too top heavy. The burden of pensions on the taxes of the working population will be onerous. By then there may well be some sort of savings plan in place, of course, but it will need to be funded and one way or another is a tax on the economy. There are many economies where the picture already looks worse now than it will in India in 50 years' time.

Japan is one of the countries at the forefront of changing demographic trends. Its population is expected to peak in 2006 and the UN Population Division estimates that by 2050 its population will have shrunk by 14%. It is not the only country likely to see its population falling in absolute terms. The UN estimates that over the next 50 years, 31 countries will have smaller populations than today, with Russia facing the largest potential fall of 50%.

### Russia's demographic time bomb

Russia's population is forecast to halve over the next 50 years. This is because the country is experiencing only one side of the demographic transition. Fertility rates fell sharply in the early 1990s but there has not been a commensurate fall in the mortality rate. Russia has the lowest life expectancy among the developed countries. In 1970 life expectancy at birth was 70, but between 1995 and 2000 it fell to 66.1

and is not expected to regain the 1970 level until 2025–30. The high level of vodka consumption not only affects the population's health – it also causes a large number of fatal accidents. A failure to tackle the growing spread of AIDS is also contributing to the high mortality rate.

## The economic consequences of ageing populations

The combination of falling fertility and mortality rates will give rise to a dramatic shift in the ratio of elderly people to those of working age. For the world as a whole, the ratio of people aged 65 or over to that of people aged 15–64 is forecast to rise from 11:100 in 2000 to 25:100 in 2050. In more developed regions the ratio will rise from 21:100 to 44:100, and in less developed regions from 7:100 to 22:100.

The rise in elderly dependency ratios is likely to have an adverse impact on economic growth, particularly in countries where the demographic transition is already fairly well entrenched. The IMF has estimated that in the developed world, falls in the working-age population could be responsible for reducing annual real GDP per head by an average of half a percentage point by 2050 (although, as the IMF points out, this does not mean that real growth will fall by this amount because other factors influencing growth will also change over this period and these may more than compensate for the negative demographic effect.)

In parts of the world where the elderly dependency ratio is rising, a larger share of government budgets will have to be allocated to services for older people, such as pension provision and health care. The difficulty encountered by governments seeking to raise the pension age is a sign of the problems that lie ahead. Introducing policies to try to limit the fiscal consequences of ageing populations raises other interesting political questions. The combination of a growing number of older voters and the fact that people over 50 are more likely to exercise their right to vote than younger people will give older people considerable political clout, making it difficult to introduce reforms that will limit their financial benefits. (For a detailed discussion of the growing political clout of the elderly see S.H. Preston's article "Children and the elderly: Divergent paths for America's dependents" in *Demography*.)

An ageing population is likely to have significant financial implications, quite apart from the fiscal consequences of higher pension and health-care costs. The life cycle theory of savings and investment postulates that to try to smooth out consumption over their lifetime, people tend to borrow when they are young, save when they are at the height of their earning capacity in middle age and then run down their savings in old age. In a society with a large proportion of middle-aged people, therefore, the level of savings will be high, driving down interest rates. But in a society with a high elderly dependency ratio the supply of savings will fall, pushing up interest rates.

The rise in the dependency ratio could have a similar effect on stockmarkets as an ageing population will sell its holding of stocks. Studies of the US stockmarket, for example, have shown a positive correlation between its performance and the proportion of the population that is at the peak savings period (40–64 years). Although a positive correlation does not necessarily imply causality, there is an intuitive logic behind this relationship.

Some analysts have questioned the assumptions underlying this life cycle of investment and savings, in particular the extent to which old people divest their savings. Uncertainty about life expectancy together with a desire to pass on wealth to future generations is likely, it is argued, to mean that older people will want to retain a proportion of their savings. But the argument centres on the rate at which savings are used up, not the direction of the trend. Once people retire from paid employment, they are unlikely to be able to continue to build up savings and most will have to dip into them. Therefore in countries with a large and rising elderly population savings will decline.

## Spending surges

The assumption that people smooth out consumption over their lifetime is a simplification in one respect – consumption patterns do fluctuate over a person's lifetime. The first surge in spending occurs, on average, around the age of 25 when individuals leave home and start buying the consumer goods that are needed to set up their own home. The decade between 40 and 50 is generally the period when they spend the most, particularly if they have children. At this stage they will own their largest house, buy their biggest car and will be funding their children through school and college. The relative size of the population in the 45–49 age group is, therefore, an important factor when assessing the impact of demographic trends on the stockmarket. (In his book *The Great Boom Ahead*, Harry S. Dent identifies 46 as the age at which the average person spends the most.)

## The baby boomers

The effect on the North American economy of the "baby boom" generation in the United States and Canada reaching the high-spending period of their lives was clear in the 1990s. The baby boomers are the bulge generation born between 1946 and 1964. Demographers have referred to this large generation as "a pig passing through a python". At each stage of their lives baby boomers have driven the economy. When they reached their mid-20s and needed starter homes, there was a surge in house building; when they needed schools, this sector of the economy boomed. By the 1990s, the baby boomers were coming into the high-spending decade of their lives and were the driving force behind the huge rise in consumer spending which, in turn, underpinned the equity market. As a string of financial problems unfolded, such as the Russian debt crisis, the Asian financial crash and the collapse of the Long-Term Capital Management hedge fund, investors nervously held their breath to see if the baby boomers would rein back their spending. But with their children going through school and college and a large mortgage to pay off, they were locked into a pattern of spending that could not easily be disrupted.

The offspring of the baby boomers have become known as the "echo generation". Although this generation is not nearly as large as that of its parents, it will nevertheless create a small demographic bulge of those born between 1977 and 1994.

Other countries experienced much smaller baby booms than the United States and Canada. In the aftermath of the destruction of the second world war, morale was low in western Europe and Japan (where the exploding of the atom bomb had a particularly devastating impact on the national psyche). Consequently, their baby booms did not start until 1950.

## Migration

The shrinking labour force in the more advanced countries is likely to encourage further economic migration from less-developed parts of the world. The UN anticipates that over the next few decades these countries will receive 2m migrants (net) annually. But only in the United States, which is expected to assimilate 1.1m immigrants a year, is immigration likely to be of sufficient size to have a significant impact on the size of the working-age population. Germany is expected to be the second largest recipient, with an inflow of 211,000, followed by Canada (173,000), the UK (136,000) and Australia (83,000). The largest emigration is likely to be from China (303,000), followed by Mexico (267,000), India (222,000), the Philippines (184,000) and Indonesia (180,000). (These figures are based on official figures and may be an underestimate given the rise in unofficial migration.)

Immigration can help boost the working-age population of a country but only temporarily since immigrants age too. However, a steadily increasing level of migration could have some impact on demographic trends, although it is unlikely to be significant enough to reverse the current patterns.

## Varying effect of demographic trends

When considering the influence of demographic factors, it is important to remember that predicting population trends is an inexact science. Past attempts have failed to anticipate fully the decline in fertility rates, for example. But future fertility levels are not a major consideration for investors trying to map out the economic and financial consequences of demographic trends over the next couple of decades, since those entering the labour market over this period have already been born. What could disrupt demographic patterns abruptly in coming decades is the outbreak of an epidemic which pushes up mortality rates. The devastating effect of the spread of HIV/AIDS on the working-age population of Sub-Saharan Africa provides a sharp reminder of what can happen when a fatal epidemic takes hold in a population. In the seven worst affected countries, the overall population is expected to grow from 74m in 2000 to only 78m in 2050; and in Botswana, Lesotho, South Africa and Swaziland population numbers are expected to continue to fall over the next 50 years.

Demographic changes do, therefore, have an important bearing on long-term secular trends, and whether their impact is negative or positive will vary considerably from region to region. Some parts of the world are rapidly approaching the point at which their working-age population begins to decline, while many areas of the developing world are likely to see the size of their working-age population rise strongly for several decades before the ageing effect sets in.

Japan is likely to be the country where growth is most affected by negative demographics, followed by central and western Europe. The areas of the world best placed to take advantage of favourable demographic trends are Africa, the Middle East and Central Asia. But in all these regions, especially Africa, it will be necessary to build the appropriate institutional framework and to develop good governance in order to take advantage of the opportunities presented by their positive demographics.

# 7 Energy

The world's demand for energy will rise sharply over the next two decades. The International Energy Agency forecasts that consumption of energy will double by 2030. Not only will the catch-up economies require vast amounts of power to effect their economic transition, but western countries' increasing reliance on ever more sophisticated technology will also underpin a steady rise in demand for energy.

There are two problems with the world's dependence on fossil fuels. The obvious one is that they will eventually run out. Previous alarms about exhausting supplies have proved premature as increasingly sophisticated equipment has led to more oil reserves being discovered, and the rise in the price of oil in recent years has made it economic to bring on stream sources of fuel that were not commercially viable to extract at lower prices. But the supply is finite, and during this century fossil fuels are likely to run out.

The second problem is the effect that burning fossil fuels has on the environment. Considerable uncertainty surrounds the science of global warming. The extent to which it is a man-made phenomenon rather than the result of natural development remains a matter of controversy. But it is generally accepted that human activity contributes to the scale of the problem.

In environmental terms, industrialisation goes through two stages. The first is best summed up by the Soviet Union's old maxim "Produce first, live later". In the initial rush to build infrastructure, cities and basic industries, scant attention is paid to the pollution that is generated. But in the second stage, as a society gets richer, greater emphasis is placed on having a clean environment. Almost every country in the world is now tightening up its environmental regulations. Even in China, where all the emphasis has been on economic development, measures are being introduced to reduce air pollution.

The demand for energy coupled with the trend towards ecological improvement has important implications for two big industries: power generation and car manufacturing.

## Power generation

Considerable research and investment has gone into trying to develop alternative sources of energy, such as solar and hydroelectric power, tidal, wave and wind energy, and biomass fuel. But the drawback with all of them (with the possible exception of solar power) is that they are just tinkering with the problem. They are not capable of producing sufficiently large quantities to meet the whole of the world's existing energy needs, let alone the much larger amounts of electricity that will be needed as economic development progresses in the catch-up countries. They may, together with improvements in energy conservation, represent a useful contribution to the overall problem, especially in the short to medium term, but they are not the ultimate solution. Even solar energy, which perhaps could be the ultimate solution, is too far away from being economic to be a clear candidate. This has led to a reassessment of nuclear power as an energy provider.

### The nuclear option

Nuclear power has always been controversial. In countries such as Sweden and more recently Germany, public opinion was so strongly opposed to it that their governments were obliged to start phasing out nuclear power as a source of electricity generation, though even in these countries opinion has begun to shift and phase-out plans have been deferred. Nuclear power stations emit only a small amount of carbon dioxide, and although the mining and processing of uranium ore, as currently practised, produces a certain amount of carbon dioxide, the amounts are small compared with stations that burn fossil fuels. So on this criterion they score highly as a clean means of producing energy. Their main drawback is that they produce highly radioactive waste and the safety of the current means of disposing of it is still controversial. It is likely that, in the long run, the waste will be buried in deep underground vaults in stable geological formations, but it is proving difficult to get public acceptance for any specific location. In the UK, for example, waste is being stored in temporary sites until an independent group decides on the most appropriate location for long-term storage.

Accidents at Three Mile Island in the United States and Chernobyl in Ukraine, as well as leaks from the UK's Sellafield nuclear power station, heightened public concerns about the safety of nuclear energy. But a new generation of reactors is being designed which will be much safer than the old ones and should help allay public fears about the risks associated with this source of energy creation. The pebble bed modular reactor, for example, is designed to withstand extremely high temperatures, thereby reducing the risk of a "meltdown" accident. The fuel is introduced into the reactor in the form of round pebbles rather than rods, which had to be taken out and replaced. New pebbles can be stacked on top of old ones, obviating the need to stop the reactor for refuelling. The process is more efficient than in the old high-temperature gas-cooled reactors so there is much less radioactive residue. There will be a specially designed hold for used pebbles underneath the reactor where they will be kept for 40 years. Some energy experts have questioned the wisdom of building a new generation of reactors powered by uranium when there are already concerns that supplies of the metal will run out. But the problem may be overstated, for two reasons:

- The prospect of a new source of demand is likely to spur exploration for new deposits. Kazakhstan, for example, produces 9.4% of the global output of uranium and plans to develop seven new mines, overtaking Canada and Australia to become the world's largest producer by 2010.
- The development of fast-breeder nuclear reactors will, in the long term, dramatically improve the utilisation of the uranium. The present nuclear reactors convert only about 1% of uranium's potential energy into "usable" energy, whereas the fast-breeder reactors will convert almost 100%. This vast improvement in utilisation will make it economic to use much lower-grade uranium ores, and hence enormously increase the world's usable reserves.

The points discussed above may well prompt a reassessment of nuclear power as a source of fuel.

## Nuclear fusion and mining the moon

Both the old and the new nuclear reactors rely on nuclear fission to generate energy. The really radical innovation would be a move to nuclear fusion. The Culham Science Centre in the UK has been leading research into fusing two isotopes of hydrogen – deuterium and tritium – at temperatures of around 100m degrees in order to produce energy. Clearly, there are practical problems associated with the commercial development of a source of energy which has to operate at such a high temperature. It is also recognised that there is some radioactive by-product from a reactor using this particular fusion reaction, although it is much less than that produced by an equivalent nuclear fission reactor, and it also has a relatively short half-life of the order of 50 years. Its disposal should therefore present much less of a problem than the radioactive waste generated by existing nuclear power plants.

Research is being carried out in the United States into a different type of fusion reaction, which produces even less radioactive waste, though it operates at an even higher temperature. This is the fusion reaction of helium-3 (an isotope of helium) with deuterium. One problem with this fuel technology is that there are only tiny amounts of helium-3 on Earth. However, in their paper "Astrofuel – An Energy Source for the 21st Century", J.F. Santarius and G.L. Kulcinski estimate that the moon has about 1m tons of helium-3, enough to meet the world's primary energy needs for over 1,000 years. How mineral deposits on the moon might be used to generate electricity on Earth is beyond the scope of this book. But it does illustrate that alternative sources of energy are available – even if the technology has not yet been developed to exploit them.

It will be seen from this superficial trawl through technologies that are currently being developed that, except in the very short term, high oil prices should not impede economic growth. Instead, they are likely to encourage research into and investment in new technologies that will allow the catch-up economies to establish a low-cost, low-carbon system of power generation.

### The great car economy

What Lady Thatcher once described as the "great car economy" brings enormous benefits to individuals, but for economies as a whole there are significant negative externalities. There are already too many cars in the western world; from the Los Angeles freeway to London's M25 motorway to the centre of Rome the roads are clogged. Many families run two or even three cars. Growing wealth in countries such as India and China will lead to a dramatic surge in demand for cars. The UN Environmental Programme estimates that there could be 200m new cars – twice the number currently on the road in the United States – if car ownership in India, Indonesia and China reaches the global average. Nowhere is this trend more evident than on the gridlocked roads of Beijing, where car fumes add to the permanent thick smog that hangs over the city. The switch from bicycles to cars as the main means of transport has been so rapid that it has forced one of the country's largest cycle manufacturers, China Bicycle, into bankruptcy.

Aware of the detrimental environmental impact of moving to a car-based economy, the Chinese authorities are planning to limit the damage by introducing a range of quality standards for car engines that will eventually be more exacting than those prevailing in the United States. But with car ownership set to double by 2020, this will do little to improve the underlying problem. Cars account for about one-third of China's annual energy consumption, and as the number of cars doubles, so will the demand for energy to fuel them.

One technological innovation that has already reached the market is the hybrid car, which runs mainly on petrol but has an electric battery that is charged up while driving along and can then be used to drive an electric motor to power the vehicle in slow-moving traffic. Although much cleaner and more efficient than the traditional internal combustion engine, these cars still produce carbon emissions. Car manufacturers are being encouraged to start producing these hybrid cars for the Chinese market. However, in the long run, a more radical solution is needed if China and other catch-up economies are to become car-based economies. The answer is another technological innovation: the fuel cell.

The fuel cell is a battery powered by hydrogen which, when mixed with oxygen from the air, produces electricity. The only by-product is hot water, so from an environmental perspective it is the perfect fuel source. Fuel cells could also be used to heat houses and water. Eventually, every home may have its own energy station that will provide all a household's energy needs, but most of the development work is focused on using the technology to power cars.

The most difficult problem with the fuel cell is how to store the hydrogen that powers the car. Storage in a high-pressure cylinder – the only proven method – means the "fuel tank" is so heavy and bulky that it can only be used in a bus. Several other lighter and cheaper approaches are being explored, but none has yet reached the market. Even when it does, the initial cost of a fuel-cell car is likely to be high, perhaps as high as the existing fuel-cell buses (around $1m each). However, Toyota, a Japanese car producer, estimates that by 2015 the price will have dropped to $50,000. General Motors is much more aggressive in its pricing target; it is aiming to cut the cost to $5,000 in just five years, although it does not envisage starting mass production as early as this.

Even when the problems associated with storing and filling up cars with hydrogen are resolved, a hydrogen distribution system will need to be set up before cars powered purely by fuel cells can be sold commercially. A number of US states are beginning to develop hydrogen-filling networks. As with so many new ideas, California is leading the way. Arnold Schwarzenegger, the state's governor, promised in 2004 to have a "hydrogen highway" in operation by 2010. However, until the best means of storing the hydrogen on board has been identified, such initiatives may be premature.

### High energy prices should spur innovation

The imbalance between the rapid surge in demand and the supply of immediately accessible oil and gas has driven prices sharply higher. A few years ago most economists would have predicted that an oil price of $60 a barrel would have tipped the global economy into recession. There are several reasons why the high price of energy has not, so far, acted as more of a drag on economic activity:

- The demand stemming from industrialisation is much less sensitive to changes in the price of oil than the cyclical demand of a mature economy.
- The global economy can produce much more economic output per barrel of oil than in the 1980s and 1970s when rises in the price of oil brought on recessions.
- Higher energy costs have occurred against a background of subdued inflationary pressures elsewhere in the economy and higher oil prices have not yet fed through to inflationary expectations – perhaps because they are expected to be temporary.

These mitigating factors have limitations, however, and if oil prices were to climb significantly above $70 a barrel they would, eventually, have a negative impact on global growth.

The longer-term consequence of higher energy costs will be to stimulate the development of replacement technologies for power generation and cars. Sheikh Yamani reportedly said that "the stone age didn't end because we ran out of stones", and the fossil fuel era is not likely to end because we run out of fossil fuels. New technology will provide cleaner, cheaper fuel for the global economy. The industrial processes and manufacturing companies that will be needed to deliver this new technology will be one of the forces that will give an upward impetus to the long-term cycle.

# 8 Biotechnology

In its broadest definition, biotechnology involves producing new drugs and medical treatments for human, animal and plant life. As far back as 20,000BC there is evidence that some members of society had a specialised role in treating those members who fell ill. A cave painting on the walls of the Grotto of Trois Frères in the Pyrenees, for instance, shows a doctor dressed in animal skins. For primitive man, illnesses were the work of demons and the doctor dressed up in the hide of a large animal such as a bear to drive away the evil spirits and also to distract patients from their ailments. It was the Greeks, however, who made the transition from faith healing to using drugs either to cure a disease or to treat the symptoms by, for example, using opium to suppress pain. As our knowledge of the human body has increased, so has the effectiveness of the remedies used to treat illnesses, injuries and medical conditions. But the major breakthrough in medical science came in 2000 when Celera Genomics and the Human Genome Project published the *Book of Life*, in which they mapped out the complete sequence of the human genome. The number of medical advances that will develop from this knowledge is huge.

## Molecular medicine

Unravelling the make-up of the human genome has led to a much greater understanding of the molecular changes that occur in certain diseases. A new science – genomics – has sprung up to study genes and the way they behave. Before the Human Genome Project's sequencing of the human genome it was thought that it would contain at least 100,000 genes, but it is now believed there are only around 25,000. However, each gene can express several proteins, which means that there could be around 500,000 proteins and variants of proteins in the human body. This has given rise to another large body of research into proteins, known as proteomics. Protein irregularities can also be treated by using specific drugs. At present, drugs are aimed at relatively few molecules in the body, but as scientists' knowledge about the function of proteins grows so will the number of targets that can be treated.

Extensive medical research is being directed towards producing antibody drugs that can target specific molecules, particularly those in cancerous cells. This not a new idea – research into the concept of developing antibodies to pinpoint individual molecules started in the 1970s – but the antibodies were produced in mice and often resulted in allergic reactions when used to treat humans. Now scientists can breed mice with an immune system similar to that found in humans so this problem has been largely overcome, paving the way for the development of "smart" drugs that can target the molecular changes that cause a normal cell to become cancerous. These drugs can be used to treat specific diseased molecules, but scientists are seeking to make them even more effective by attaching toxic chemicals to the antibodies which can, for example, attack solid tumours.

It is estimated that the amount of genetic information being discovered is doubling every six months. New computing techniques have had to be developed to cope with this vast outpouring of information, giving rise to yet another new field of research – bioinformatics – which harnesses computer technology to the rapidly growing databank of genetic information. The body of medical/information technology specialities that have sprung up will eventually revolutionise medical science. But it is important to emphasise that this will not be an instant revolution; there has already been some frustration that the discovery of the make-up of the human genome has not yielded more immediate medical – and financial – benefits.

The gestation period between discovering a new drug and launching it commercially can often be more than ten years. A new drug has to go through a rigorous testing procedure. After the initial research and development, it then goes through clinical trials. During phase 1, the drug is tested on healthy volunteers. At this stage it has a 20% chance of going through to the phase 2 trials, when it is tested on patients with the particular disease or condition that it is designed to cure or alleviate. On average, about 30% of drugs pass this test and go on to phase 3, which involves long-term trials aimed at picking up adverse side-effects that arise from prolonged use. Once the drug has passed successfully through these trials, approval can be sought from the relevant authority, such as the Food and Drug Administration in the United States or the Medicine and Healthcare Products Regulatory Agency in the UK, but even at this stage it is by no means certain that it will be given. Approximately 25% of drugs fail at the phase 3 stage, and for some treatments the percentage is much higher.

New technology should truncate the testing process because scientists will be able to predict the effect of drugs on humans using genomic tools.

In this way potential problems should be picked up at a much earlier stage, obviating the need to go through costly clinical trials.

## Personalised medicine

Managing such an explosion of new data presents its own problems. Correlating and cross-referencing all the data emanating from the study of human genetics is a laborious task, and the "absorption" period during which scientists try to understand the complex relationships between the human genome and diseases is taking longer than was initially envisaged. Eventually, however, medicine will become much more personalised.

Genetic profiling will allow doctors to predict which patients will be susceptible to certain diseases and what treatments are likely to be most efficient at treating or alleviating their condition. For example, Herceptin, a drug used to treat advanced cases of breast cancer, is successful only in patients whose tumours overexpress the gene HER-2 and is, therefore, appropriate for only 25–30% of patients with this form of cancer.

### *Increasing computerisation*

The contribution that advances in computer technology will make to medical science is not just limited to processing data. Surgeons are being trained to operate using computer simulators in the same way that pilots are trained on flight simulators and robots have been developed which are already carrying out some surgical procedures. Oklahoma Heart Hospital claims to be the first hospital in the United States to operate completely electronically. Any paper records that a patient may have are scanned into a computer and thereafter all records – including X-rays – are stored electronically. The switch to computerising patient records is well under way (though not without problems in the UK).

### *Nanotechnology opens up a new frontier of medicine*

Decades from now, the interaction between molecular biology and nanotechnology will open up a new frontier of medical treatment. Tiny molecular-sized nanomachines are being developed that will be able to ferry drugs to specific parts of the body that require repair or treatment. Scientists are also building nanocomputers so small that 10,000 of them can be contained within a single drop of fluid. Eventually, one of these computers will be injected into an individual's blood stream and will travel around the body making an internal diagnosis. The results of the diagnosis will probably then be relayed to a larger computer near the patient which will process the information and, if necessary, send a prescription to the pharmacy. Future generations may come to regard the job of a doctor who sits down and discusses patients' symptoms and medical history with them as a historical curiosity – in the same way as we now regard Victorian lamplighters.

### A clustering of life science innovations

The revolution that is occurring in the life sciences is a good illustration of Joseph Schumpeter's theory that innovations tend to fan out across an economy. The sequencing of the human genome has spawned new branches of science. The advances in medical knowledge brought about by these technologies will be enormous, but they will also raise difficult social and ethical issues. Targeted drug treatments are likely to be expensive because the research and development costs cannot be spread over such a large cohort of patients as they can with a blockbuster drug such as Zantac (used to treat and prevent ulcers in the stomach and intestines). For example, one year's treatment with Herceptin, the breast cancer drug mentioned above, costs $43,000 (£25,000). Governments and health authorities will have to make increasingly difficult decisions about which drugs and treatments they are able to supply to people who cannot fund the cost of treatment themselves. Will insurance companies insist on genetic screening before issuing health cover and even refuse to cover people with genotypes that make them susceptible to heart disease? Stem cell research also raises controversial questions. But notwithstanding these ethical issues, this new revolution in medicine is unstoppable, and the cluster of innovations and new developments that result will make a beneficial contribution to the long-term trend of growth.

### Summary

In terms of economic development, over half the world's population is still in the early stages of industrialisation. The impact of this economic transition will be far-reaching. Increasing demand for scarce raw materials will drive up prices. But just as Thomas Malthus was wrong to see population growth as a limiting factor on economic growth, so the rising cost of raw materials will not (except in the very short term) curb growth. Rather, it will stimulate research and development into alternative technologies. Furthermore, the trend towards replacement technologies will be given added impetus by the catch-up countries. As their economies become richer, there will be greater focus on the environmental consequences of economic growth. More resources will then be devoted to research and implementation of cleaner energy and less dependence on scarce resources.

Just as the development of the railway engine opened up new physical frontiers, so the development of scientific technology to treat diseases at the molecular level and below has opened up new frontiers of medicine. The economic consequences of these developments will have a strong, positive impact on longer-term secular trends.

# PART 3
# DOWNWARD PHASES OF THE CYCLE

Implicit in cycle analysis is the assumption that there will be downward phases to the cycle as well as upward ones. This reflects the natural world where periods of growth are followed by periods of rest during which energy is replenished. The extent of the downward phase of a cycle will depend on the strength and duration of the upward phase. It will also depend on the extent to which the diversion of resources to take advantage of the upswing has disrupted the economic equilibrium and created a bubble. If growth, valuations or prices are stretched too far, like a piece of elastic they will snap back with a vicious "ping". The ping factor will vary according to the circumstances behind the creation of the bubble. For example, the bursting of the internet bubble in technology stocks in 2000 resulted in a two-year bear market and caused only a shallow recession in the United States (though some argue that the Federal Reserve's actions to truncate the recession prevented the correction of other imbalances in the economy). Yet the collapse of Japan's asset bubble consigned the economy to a decade and a half of zero growth in real terms and a similarly long downturn in the stockmarket, during which the market's capitalisation dropped to less than a quarter of its 1989 value.

There is a view that more sophisticated financial monitoring and a readiness by central banks to take pre-emptive action (such as the dramatic monetary easing carried out by the US Federal Reserve in 2000–03) has made prolonged recessions a thing of the past. Economic growth may pause, it is argued, but economies will not experience the type of severe downtrend envisaged in the Kondratieff cycle. Other analysts are convinced that the longer a major downturn is delayed, the more severe it will be when it does finally come. Like the Bank of Japan in the 1990s, central banks will be powerless to prevent the onset of what is sometimes referred to as an "economic winter".

# 9 Global imbalances

## US current-account deficit

There are a number of major imbalances in the global economy. The one that provokes most comment is the US current-account deficit. As Figure 9.1 shows, apart from a brief blip in 1991, the US current account has been in deficit since the early 1980s, and over the past decade there has been a marked deterioration in the trend.

Normally, when a country runs a current-account balance the currency comes under pressure and real interest rates rise, tilting the balance of growth away from the domestic economy and towards the export sector. But the United States has managed to defy the normal laws of economics by virtue of the fact that the dollar is the international reserve currency. During the 1990s, the negative flows across the US balance of payments on the current account were more than offset by the inflows on the capital account. Foreign investors were keen to buy American assets and overseas companies were busy acquiring American businesses. During the bear market of 2000–03 these capital inflows fell away. The currency came under pressure between 2002 and 2004, but it did not fall by as much as might be expected given the size of the current-account deficit. The reason

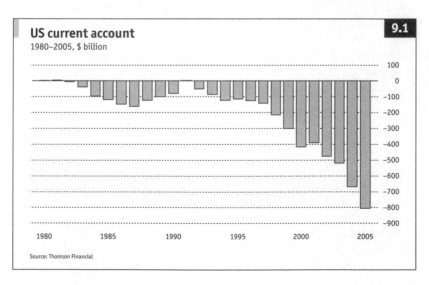

**US current account**
1980–2005, $ billion

Source: Thomson Financial

9.1

for this is that another source of dollar buyers stepped into the market – the Asian central banks.

## High saving ratios in Asia

A number of analysts including Ben Bernanke, chairman of the Fed, have characterised the imbalance on the US current account as not so much a problem of a lack of savings in the United States as a glut of savings elsewhere, particularly in the Asian economies. The effect of these central banks buying up US Treasury bonds and bills has been to keep long-term US interest rates artificially low.

## An unsustainable imbalance

From whichever perspective the US current-account deficit is viewed, most analysts agree that an imbalance of this size, which is continuing to deteriorate, cannot be sustained indefinitely. It will require a global solution. In 1985, a similar problem was resolved by the Plaza Accord, whereby the G7 finance ministers agreed to intervene to reduce the dollar's value, among other measures. By the end of 1987 the dollar had depreciated by 54% against both the D-mark and the yen from its peak in 1985. The move succeeded in reducing the current-account deficit from 3.4% of GDP in 1985 to 1.4% in 1990. This time around the problem is slightly different. At an estimated 6.4% of GDP, the deficit is double what it was in the 1980s, and much of the counterpart to it lies in the emerging Asian economies and, since the sharp rise in the oil price, the oil-exporting countries. The Asian countries have large trade surpluses, but for political reasons they are reluctant to implement the appropriate policies to bring them down. Essentially, what is required is for the US savings rate to rise, the dollar to depreciate and domestic consumption in the Asian economies to be stimulated.

### Low savings ratios and house prices

Rising house prices and low savings ratios in the United States and the UK, for example, are other facets of this potentially destabilising imbalance. As Figures 9.2 and 9.3 show, in both countries savings ratios as a percentage of disposable income have been on a declining trend since 1990. In this respect, consumers have been behaving perfectly rationally in the face of rising house prices. They have realised that the capital value of their houses has been rising, so rather than making savings out of their income they have been accruing savings in the form of capital.

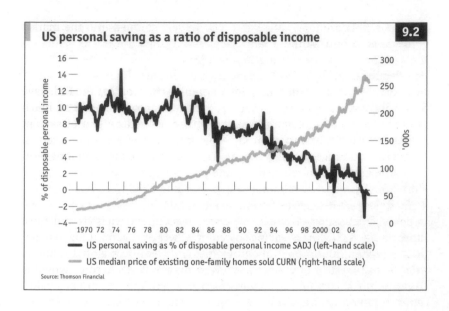

**9.2**

## US personal saving as a ratio of disposable income

— US personal saving as % of disposable personal income SADJ (left-hand scale)
— US median price of existing one-family homes sold CURN (right-hand scale)

Source: Thomson Financial

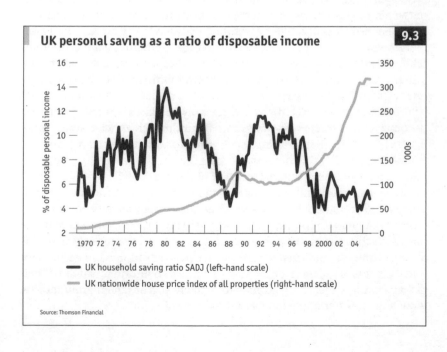

**9.3**

## UK personal saving as a ratio of disposable income

— UK household saving ratio SADJ (left-hand scale)
— UK nationwide house price index of all properties (right-hand scale)

Source: Thomson Financial

Rising house prices engender consumer confidence, prompting consumers to borrow more (and save less) against the higher value of their houses. Given the rising trend in house prices over the past two decades, the higher levels of debt incurred by households have been more than covered by the value of their property and their financial assets. Seeing the advantages of this virtuous debt cycle, new buyers have been attracted into the housing market, which has helped drive prices even higher. In turn, the buoyancy of the consumer sector prompts businesses to increase investment so incomes rise, further underpinning confidence.

A problem occurs if consumers suddenly find the store of their savings – the housing stock – beginning to lose its value. Savings levels are now so far below their long-run average that should houses no longer prove to be a safe repository for their savings, consumers would try to build up more traditional forms of savings by cutting their expenditure and setting aside a higher proportion of their income. The trend on both sides of the Atlantic to invest in buy-to-let properties means that many consumers could, without having the inconvenience of scaling down their own living accommodation, reduce their exposure to the housing market by just a phone call to their estate agent. Although this would affect only one segment of the market, the knock-on effects would quickly spread outwards to the rest of the market. In both the United States and the UK, there are signs that the housing market is cooling off and a period of consolidation would allow this imbalance to unwind gradually. But if for some reason house prices were to drop sharply, this could precipitate a sharp retrenchment in consumer spending which would have serious implications for global growth.

Economic imbalances do not necessarily result in a market crash or debt crunch. A smooth adjustment can occur through either market forces or official policies. But imbalances are easier to sustain when an economy is growing steadily. In this respect the economy is rather like riding a bicycle. If a cyclist hits a small bump or pothole once a comfortable head of speed has been built up, it is not too difficult to steady the bicycle. There may be some loss of speed while the correction is occurring, but basically the bicycle continues on in the same direction. If the same thing happens when the cyclist is moving very slowly or, alternatively, is racing ahead at full tilt, the chances are the bicycle would crash. The current imbalances will therefore pose more of a threat to financial stability if the global economy were to decelerate to a much slower rate of growth or to grow above its trend rate for a sustained period.

# 10 External events

In his book *Business Cycles: A Theoretical, Historical and Statistical Analysis of the Capitalist Process*, Joseph Schumpeter made the point that if the short-, medium- and long-term cycles are all moving in the same direction, they will tend to reinforce each other. The chances of an economy experiencing a prolonged recession or even depression are obviously greatest when the long-term and short-term cycles are both in a downward phase. But even then it is not inevitable. Greater understanding of the nature of economic cycles and more sophisticated techniques for monitoring the economy mean that central banks are better equipped to counteract the downward swing in cycles. There probably needs to be some additional external factor, which delivers a major unexpected shock to an economy, to bring on a severe downturn or "economic winter".

By definition, if a shock is to be unexpected, it is a fairly fruitless exercise to try to speculate what form that shock might take. Terrorism, wars (both trade and physical) and natural catastrophes are all possible contenders. But to illustrate their potential impact, it is worth considering two possible shocks: an influenza pandemic and a water shortage.

## Influenza pandemic

An infectious disease that spreads across a broad geographical region or even worldwide can have serious economic consequences. Even with the benefits of modern medicine, an influenza pandemic could have a negative impact on economic growth. The H5N1 strain of avian influenza may not mutate to a form that can easily be passed on to humans. But if it does, the worry is that as the virus would be carried by migrating birds, it could quickly become a global problem. Although medical science has improved almost beyond recognition since the Spanish flu pandemic of 1918–19 killed 20m–40m people, there are nevertheless still considerable logistical challenges in preventing a viral infection of this nature from spreading. As a yardstick, the 2003 outbreak of the SARS virus infected 8,000 people, of whom around 800 died. According to the Asian Development Bank (ADB), this reduced GDP for East Asia (excluding Japan) by approximately $18 billion or 0.6%.

Apart from the Spanish flu virus, there were two other flu pandemics (1957–58 and 1968–69) in the 20th century. Trying to estimate the possible economic consequences of a pandemic involves a complex range of variables but in a November 2005 report, *The Potential Economic Impact of an Avian Flu Pandemic on Asia*, the ADB looked at two possible outcomes. Both assume a mild infection rate, with 20% of the population succumbing to the virus and just 0.5% of those infected dying. The first scenario assumes that the pandemic is short-lived, seriously affecting demand for six months and having a much less severe impact in the subsequent six months. The more negative scenario assumes that demand remains seriously affected for a year. The ADB's model predicts that under the first scenario the drop in demand caused by the erosion of consumer confidence will amount to $99.2 billion or 2.3 percentage points of GDP (relative to the ADB's forecast growth rate for the region of, for example, 7.2% in 2006 and 7% in 2007); under the second scenario the contraction could rise to $282.7 billion or 6.5% of GDP. On the supply side, the economic impact of people being off work because of influenza is a much lower $14.2m (0.3% of GDP); this would be the same for both scenarios because the background infection rate assumptions are common to both.

Governments have drawn up emergency procedures to try to limit the spread of an infectious disease. These include restricting travel and trying to prevent groups of people gathering together in places of entertainment or even restaurants. Whether it is bird flu or some other virus, as the ADB model shows, a pandemic could have a marked impact on global growth.

### Water shortage

Water is essential for sustaining life, yet many in the western world take it for granted. Apart from the human body's immediate need for water, it touches on all aspects of life: food, health, energy and industry. With water covering approximately 75% of the earth's surface, a shortage is not an obvious problem. But 96.5% of the total volume of the earth's water is sea water, and some 70% of the fresh water is held in glaciers and icecaps. In the 2003 UN World Water Development Report, *Water for People, Water for Life*, it is estimated that "2 billion people are affected by water shortages in over 40 countries: 1.1 billion do not have sufficient drinking water and 2.4 billion have no provision for sanitation" (WHO/UNICEF, 2000). Even in parts of the world where there is an apparent abundance of water, the lakes and rivers are becoming increasingly polluted.

In the past 50 years the world's consumption of water has doubled. Population growth, industrialisation and increased tourism have led to a sharp rise in demand, while climate change appears to be reducing supply. The UN report is unambiguous in its conclusion: "There is a water crisis."

Without water crops fail, and hunger has been the catalyst for many uprisings and wars. A 2001 Oregon State University study estimated that there had been 1,831 disputes over water between two or more countries over the past 50 years, of which 507 involved "conflict-related events". Increasing competition for limited supplies of fresh water will inevitably cause disputes, which could easily spill over into conflict.

The two big catch-up economies, India and China, face major water shortages. In parts of India, the water table is dropping by 1–3 metres a year and many large cities are experiencing chronic water shortages. In 2004, the Indian state of Punjab informed neighbouring states that it would be cutting off their water because its farmers were short of water. Within 20 years the country as a whole is likely to face a serious water crisis. To try to help farmers, the Indian government proposed diverting water from the Ganges–Brahmaputra basin to southern and eastern parts of the country. But this would have a detrimental effect on the amount of water flowing into Bangladesh, and not surprisingly the Bangladeshi government protested vociferously about the Indian government's plans to alleviate its own water problems. In 2003, the UN set up the Water Co-operation Facility to mediate in international disputes of this nature.

In the longer term, water shortage is not likely to be a limiting factor in global growth. There is a well-established desalination industry, converting sea water into fresh water, which produces less than 1% of the world's freshwater requirement. Environmental concerns about the toxic by-products generated by this process will need to be addressed before the industry can gear up to meet a much more significant proportion of the world's water needs, but it is estimated that the desalination industry is likely to double over the next 15 years.

Eventually, desalination and improved recycling techniques could become a positive driver for the global economy. But in the medium term water shortage is a potentially negative external factor. There is a direct negative economic consequence of a shortage of water, which hits the agricultural industry hardest. The 2003 European drought, for example, is estimated to have cost $13 billion in lost crop production. But the indirect consequences could be even more damaging if increasingly fierce competition for this essential resource causes conflict.

## Summary

The onset of a severe economic downturn over the next decade is by no means inevitable, but the presence of such large imbalances in the global economy is a concern. The emergency monetary easing undertaken by the US Federal Reserve between 2001 and 2003, when short-term rates were reduced from 6.5% to 1%, together with comments made at the time, show how worried the authorities were about the prospect of the US economy succumbing to the sort of deflationary pressures that ensnared the Japanese economy for 15 years. The reason for the concern is that the risks for monetary authorities are asymmetrical. If an economy overheats and inflation starts to pick up, interest rates are an effective tool for reversing the process. But if an economy slips into deflation, once nominal interest rates reach zero there is nothing more in monetary terms that the authorities can do. (Indeed, with falling prices and interest rates at zero, real interest rates are on a rising trend.) Fiscal measures can still be introduced, but as successive stimulation packages in Japan have shown, fiscal policy is not an effective stimulus to demand when consumer confidence is in the doldrums.

If the current imbalances remain unchecked when the four-year and ten-year cycles are trending downwards in 2009–10, the global economy will be vulnerable to recessionary forces. However, even then, this vulnerability does not necessarily mean a recession will occur. Aware of the risks, the authorities will do everything they can to ward off a prolonged downturn. There will, therefore, need to be some additional catalyst to turn a normal cyclical downtrend that can be tempered by monetary policy into a vicious downward vortex that is immune to the guile of the financial authorities.

# PART 4
## TAKING MARKET BEARINGS

Strong economic growth does not always translate into a steady upward trend in a country's stockmarket. Just as a small sailing dinghy cannot make much headway when it is facing a strong prevailing wind even if it has the tide behind it, so a country on a positive secular trend will not always see its stockmarket outperforming that of other markets – even those on a negative secular trend. There are three reasons for this:

- ◪ Structural factors may impede the smooth working of the stockmarket. China falls into this category. Although the economy grew by an estimated 9.3% in 2005, the Shanghai stockmarket's index of "A" shares fell by 8.27%.
- ◪ There can be a re-evaluation of the factors linking the stockmarket with the underlying economy, such as the rating of earnings or the share of profits as a ratio of GDP.
- ◪ Profits of companies listed on one particular stockmarket are no longer merely a reflection of the performance of its domestic economy. As a result of the growing trend towards globalisation, businesses are increasingly exposed to overseas markets, and a marked downturn in a major trading partner could have an adverse impact on the performance of a stockmarket. The greater the proportion of earnings derived from overseas markets, the more a stockmarket will be affected by global growth and international events.

However, even allowing for distortions, there tends to be a positive correlation between changes in GDP growth and stockmarket perform-ance. Stockmarket uptrends in an economy on a positive secular trend will usually extend higher and downtrends will be shallower than those in a market with a strongly negative secular trend.

Mapping out the future direction of a market involves looking at the long-term secular trend, assessing the factors that link the underlying economy with the stockmarket, and lastly analysing trends within the market itself. Part 4 analyses where the major markets are in relation to

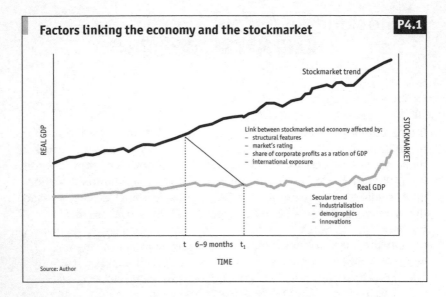

**Factors linking the economy and the stockmarket** P4.1

REAL GDP

STOCKMARKET

Stockmarket trend

Link between stockmarket and economy affected by:
- structural features
- market's rating
- share of corporate profits as a ration of GDP
- international exposure

Real GDP

Secular trend
- industrialisation
- demographics
- innovations

t    6–9 months   t₁

TIME

Source: Author

the road maps outlined in Part 1. It also looks at which sectors of these markets are likely to show outperformance.

# 11 Stockmarkets

The swing back from the West to the East began some time ago, but the huge tidal force of growth during industrialisation takes a long time to build up and it tends to occur in a series of waves or cycles. In order to move from the emerging category to a dominant economic force, an economy must achieve critical mass. Although China and India are rapidly building up this critical mass, their stockmarkets are still a long way from taking over from the United States as the global financial metronome that taps out the beat which most of the world's stockmarkets follow. Over the next decade at least, the US market will continue to set the tone for global equities, apart from in Japan, which is emerging from a 15-year downtrend and is moving according to its own recovery rhythm. The rest of the world's stockmarkets will not move exactly in synchronisation with the United States. The presidential election cycle taps out a very regular four-year beat for the US market, but elsewhere individual cycles can vary from three to five years.

## The United States

With a fertility rate close to the replacement rate of 2.1% and a large influx of immigrant workers, the population of the United States is forecast to grow by approximately 70m over the next 25 years. Overall demographic trends are, therefore, more favourable in the United States than in any other developed countries. However, the leading edge of the baby-boom generation hit the critical 45–49 age range in 2000, and by 2010 two-thirds of them will be over 50 years old.

As the large baby-boom generation falls out of the high-spending age bracket there are implications for one of the factors that links the underlying economy with the stockmarket: the rating the market attaches to earnings. (There is considerable debate among analysts about which of the various definitions of earnings provides the best corporate yardstick, but for the purposes of taking bearings as to where the stockmarket is in relation to the underlying economy, it is important to be consistent. Historic earnings are used in this book.) Strong demographic forces were one of the factors that helped push up the price/earnings (P/E) ratio in the late 1990s bubble. Like many other variables, market ratings tend to move in long-term cycles, and the experience of the 1960s provides a salutary

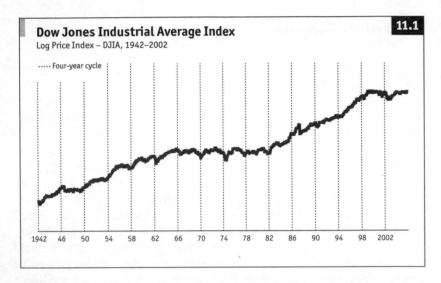

**Dow Jones Industrial Average Index**    11.1
Log Price Index – DJIA, 1942–2002

····· Four-year cycle

1942  46   50   54   58   62   66   70   74   78   82   86   90   94   98   2002

lesson as to what can happen when ratings become overly optimistic at the peak of the cycle.

As can be seen in Figure 11.1, immediately after the second world war the US stockmarket took off – this was the boom that ended in the "nifty-fifty" bubble. The reconstruction of Europe and industrialisation of Japan provided a positive secular undertow to both the economy and the market. At this time a young Warren Buffett was learning from his mentor and stockmarket guru, Benjamin Graham, and the prevailing advice was to buy a stock on a P/E ratio of 8 and sell it when the P/E ratio rose to 15. But by April 1971 the market was trading on a multiple of 20.42, highlighting the fact that there are no fixed parameters for P/E ratios.

In 1966 the Dow Jones Index hit the magic level of 1,000 – a new high watermark – before rolling back. Subsequent rallies brought the market up to this level on four separate occasions, but it never managed to break above it for a sustained period. It took four four-year cycles and some of the next bull phase (17 years in total) before the 1,000 hurdle was comprehensively cleared. As late as mid-1982, the Dow Jones was 22% lower than its peak in 1966, and in the intervening years support at 760 was tested six times. On one occasion – 1973 – this support level gave way, and from the cycle top in 1972 to the bottom in 1974 the market shed 45% of its value. Clearly, a passive buy-and-hold investment strategy over this period would have been a disaster. Even a more proactive policy would have yielded terrible results unless an

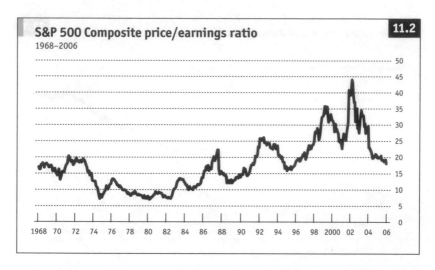

**S&P 500 Composite price/earnings ratio**
1968–2006

11.2

investor understood the cyclical nature of markets and was able to get the timing correct.

As can be seen in Figure 11.3, the Dow Jones Index traced out the pattern of bull and bear trends characteristic of a secular downtrend. The bull phase is shortened and the bear part of the cycle is relatively long, with a depressing tendency to reach lower lows (as happened in

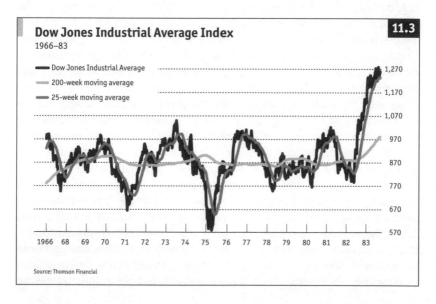

**Dow Jones Industrial Average Index**
1966–83

11.3

— Dow Jones Industrial Average
— 200-week moving average
— 25-week moving average

Source: Thomson Financial

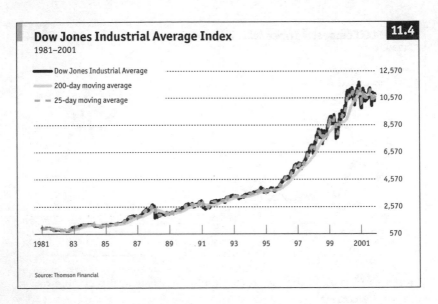

**Dow Jones Industrial Average Index**
1981–2001

11.4

— Dow Jones Industrial Average
— 200-day moving average
- - 25-day moving average

12,570
10,570
8,570
6,570
4,570
2,570
570

1981  83  85  87  89  91  93  95  97  99  2001

Source: Thomson Financial

the first three cycles). Not only did earnings hardly grow in real terms over this period, but there was also a substantial re-evaluation of the rating that the market attached to those earnings. The market's rating had become so high that there had to be some deflation of the bubble and, as can be seen in Figure 11.2 on the previous page, the P/E ratio was on a downtrend from 1971 to 1982. It did not fall in a straight line but ratcheted lower each cycle. By 1974 it was down to single figures before rallying higher, but in the next cycle it fell back again and by 1982 the market was still trading on a multiple that was a quarter of what it had been in 1966.

Spurred on by the technological revolution, a new secular uptrend got under way in 1982 and lasted until 2000. During this period, the index rose by 1,391%. The pattern of bullish and bear trends within the uptrend conformed neatly to that of a market in secular uptrend. The P/E ratio also posted new highs each cycle until it reached a peak of 46 in 2001.

It can be argued that the peak of the bubble in 2000 was reminiscent of the top of the market experienced in the late 1960s. Both periods experienced a similar build-up to the top. On the S&P 500, the boom period from 1980 to 2000 resembled the bull market from 1945 to 1966, while the bear pattern from 1968 to the low in 1970 (see Figure 11.5) was equivalent to the bear move from 2000 to late 2002 (see Figure 11.6).

There has been some correction in the P/E ratio from the 2001 peak,

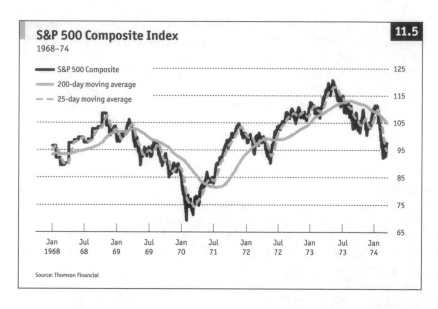

**S&P 500 Composite Index**
1968–74

11.5

— S&P 500 Composite
— 200-day moving average
- - 25-day moving average

Source: Thomson Financial

but it still remains above the trend rate of 18 and the concern is that the next downward cycle will take it well below the trend rate. US corporate profits represent a higher proportion of GDP than at any time since the 1960s, and on this criterion, too, there may be scope for some further

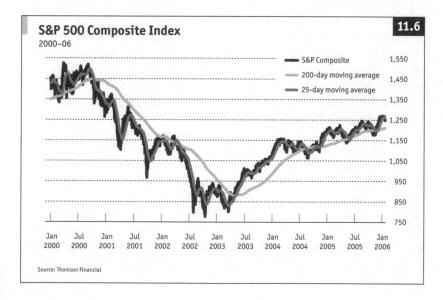

**S&P 500 Composite Index**
2000–06

11.6

— S&P Composite
— 200-day moving average
— 25-day moving average

Source: Thomson Financial

downward adjustment to the market's rating. There are also economic imbalances evident in the US economy, such as the current-account deficit, low household savings and a housing bubble (as outlined in Chapter 9). If these start unwinding, they will reinforce the downward pressure on the market's rating. If past experience is any guide, this correction process could take a number of years to work through.

Another negative on the map of the US stockmarket is that the country's manufacturing base still needs to come to terms with the industrialisation that is occurring in China and other developing countries. Companies such as General Motors, the old AT&T, US Steel and Kodak have found it difficult to meet the challenge of the changing economic landscape. New products, new methods of production and lower labour costs have given an edge to their Asian rivals, and these American giants risk becoming industrial dinosaurs. Corporate America will have to undergo a painful restructuring process as it shifts away from manufacturing industries, where developing countries enjoy a comparative advantage, to a more service-based economy.

As shown in Figure 11.1 on page 104, with the exception of 1986, the US stockmarket has barely faltered in the four-year cycle, experiencing cyclical lows in 1962, 1966, 1970, 1974, 1978, 1982, 1990, 1994, 1998 and 2002. This suggests that 2006 will be a testing year for investors. The problem for the US market is that the natural downturn of the cycles could trigger the unravelling of the imbalances that have developed within the economy. The authorities are fully aware of the background economic risks and will do everything they can to mitigate downside pressures. However, in 2010 the downturn of the four-year and ten-year cycles will coincide, and if the global imbalances have not unwound by then there could be a particularly severe bear phase of the cycle. The normal setback in a bear secular downtrend is around 25% but, in the 1973–74 shake-out, equities fell by 45%. Unless there is some additional negative external factor (such as a global epidemic of the human variant of avian flu) it is highly unlikely that, even if one of the next bear phases of the cycle turns out to be as bad as 1973–74, it will trigger the onset of an extended economic recession similar to that experienced in Japan. Although, at the time, there will no doubt be deep pessimism accompanied by dire predictions of a 1930s depression, the combined forces of industrialisation and innovation are already beginning to create a powerful undertow that will drive the next secular uptrend. Furthermore, by 2012, the echo generation (the children of the baby boomers) will be hitting the first high-spending period of their lives.

As in 1966–83, the next couple of cycles will not be a time for investors to adopt a buy-and-hold strategy; nor will it be a time to pull out of equities altogether. The market will enjoy some strong rallies, and at the appropriate time investors in stocks who are either involved in new technologies or benefiting from the industrialisation that is going on in other parts of the world will net some large returns.

## Japan

During Japan's growth phase in the 1980s there was a close correlation between the US and Japanese stockmarkets. But since the bursting of the asset bubble in 1989, this link has been severed and Japan is the only major market that has not been moving broadly in step with the US cycle.

The bubble that developed in Japanese assets during the 1980s distorted the link between the economy and the stockmarket, taking ratings to stratospheric levels (the P/E ratio on the Nikkei 225 index reached 76 in June 1987). Deflating the bubble was an extremely protracted process because of structural inefficiencies in the economy (see page 17). Negative demographics (see Chapter 6) will put this economy back on a secular downtrend, but there may be a short of stay of execution while Japan's albeit rather small baby-boom generation remains in the labour force; they will begin to retire in 2010.

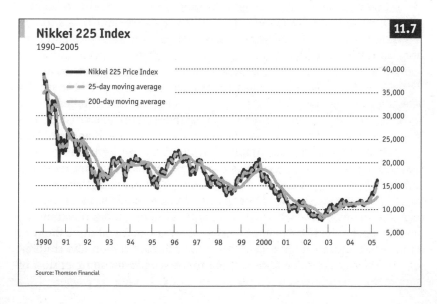

**Nikkei 225 Index**     11.7
1990–2005

Nikkei 225 Price Index
25-day moving average
200-day moving average

Source: Thomson Financial

In the short term, the economy's emergence from its 15-year hibernation is likely to drive the stockmarket higher. Japan has the second largest stockmarket in the world, yet for much of the past decade and a half international fund managers have kept their holdings of Japanese shares to a minimum. When the market started to recover in 2005, they scrambled to restore a more appropriate weighting to this large market. Over the next few years, bullish phases of the cycle may be much stronger than those usually associated with a market in secular downtrend as international investors continue to rebuild their exposure to the Japanese market. This catch-up effect will be even more pronounced if domestic investors return to the market, but once the buying spree has run its course Japan is likely to underperform most other stockmarkets.

## UK

The baby boom in the UK was nothing like as large as that experienced in North America, so there will not be the same economic deceleration as there will be in the United States when this generation moves out of its high-spending years. But the negative effect of an ageing population will, eventually, have an adverse economic impact. In the medium term, the UK economy is well placed to face the challenges that industrialisation of the lesser-developed economies will inevitably bring to the western world.

UK manufacturers experienced a bruising shake-out in the 1980s and there has been a big shift to a more service-based economy. Historical associations with East Asia have also enabled companies to build up commercial links with this fast-growing part of the world fairly easily. A significant number of the largest UK companies are involved in the commodity markets or sectors of the market that are at the forefront of technological change.

At 15 the market's rating is just above the long-term trend rate of 14, and it is likely to be the UK's economic exposure to the United States, rather than domestic factors, that drags it lower. Weighted by market value, about a quarter of UK companies pay their dividends in dollars, reflecting either dependence on US earnings or the nature of their business. Not surprisingly, therefore, the UK stockmarket marches to the same rhythm as the US market, although sometimes with a slight time lag. For example, the US market bottomed out in October 2002, whereas the low point in the UK occurred six months later in March 2003. Given this reliance on the US economy, the UK market cannot remain impervious to any correction experienced on the other side of the Atlantic. However, given

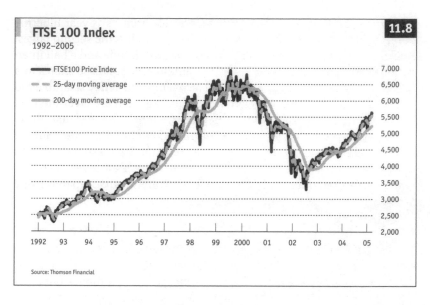

**FTSE 100 Index**
1992–2005

11.8

— FTSE100 Price Index
— 25-day moving average
— 200-day moving average

7,000
6,500
6,000
5,500
5,000
4,500
4,000
3,500
3,000
2,500
2,000

1992  93  94  95  96  97  98  99  2000  01  02  03  04  05

Source: Thomson Financial

the structure of the UK economy, any cyclical downturn is likely to be followed by strong upward rallies.

## Europe

Europe's negative demographics are compounded by structural problems. In the EU, politicians have not got the blueprint for project "United Europe" right. The one-size-fits-all monetary policy is proving uncomfortable for countries in the euro area that are not performing in line with the majority, while the Stability and Growth Pact is in disarray after Germany, the prime mover behind this policy, was one of the first to break its rules.

With its huge manufacturing base, a country like Germany faces a direct challenge from East Asia's growing industrialisation. Fidelity International compiled a league table of the top ten European multinationals (excluding UK companies) by market capitalisation in 1985 and 2005. In 1985 seven of the top ten businesses were German, but in 2005 not a single German company appeared in the list. Switzerland, which had only one company listed in 1985, boasted four companies in 2005. Although the listings reflect some merger and takeover activity (for example, Daimler Benz merged with Chrysler and Hoechst was acquired by Sanofi-Aventis), the change over the past decade illustrates succinctly the problems facing the German corporate sector as heavy engineering loses out to competition from East

111

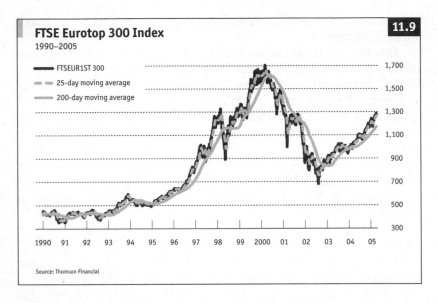

**FTSE Eurotop 300 Index**     `11.9`
1990–2005

- FTSEUR1ST 300
- 25-day moving average
- 200-day moving average

1,700
1,500
1,300
1,100
900
700
500
300

1990  91  92  93  94  95  96  97  98  99  2000  01  02  03  04  05

Source: Thomson Financial

Asia. It also highlights the increasing importance of the pharmaceuticals and telecommunications sectors.

To benefit from the industrialisation of the catch-up economies, European countries must be dynamic and create intellectual capital through innovation. Even the European Commission accepts that the EU lags well behind the United States and Japan in this respect. It has developed a European Innovation Scoreboard (EIS) which compares the level of innovation in the 25 EU member countries as well as Bulgaria, Romania, Turkey, Iceland, Norway, Switzerland, the United States and Japan. According to the 2005 EIS, there is considerable disparity among European states, with Sweden, Finland and Switzerland the front-runners when it comes to innovation. The Commission's report concludes that if current trends for the 25 EU member states remain stable, the gap with the United States will not close within the next 50 years. Meanwhile, the gap between the 25 EU members and Japan is increasing. One of the reasons Europe is slow to embrace change and innovation is that its regulatory environment is not conducive to the culture of risk-taking and starting up new enterprises. The problems that the French government has encountered in trying to change the country's employment laws in order to reduce the high levels of youth unemployment are a good example of the intransigence often found in "old Europe".

Europe as a whole may be on a negative road map, but some countries, such as Norway (which is not part of the EU) where the oil sector is such a dominant feature of the economy, are likely to show strong outperformance.

Although the European stockmarkets will follow the broad direction of the US market, there is less correlation than there used to be because around three-quarters of Europe's trade is now between other European countries. The FTSE Eurotop 300 index was slow to regain 50% of the ground lost from its 2000 peak, so like the Japanese market, there may still be a little more "catch-up element" left to run in terms of relative performance against other major indices, especially as since 2000 a surge of mergers and acquisitions has triggered a shake-up of the corporate sector. But any sell-off in New York will result in extended bear trends in the European indices, which are likely to be followed by weak rebounds during the bullish phases of the cycle.

## China

Booming economic growth has not fed through to China's stockmarket. The massive overhang of non-tradable shares held by the state has acted like a ball and chain on share prices. An investment of $100 in Shanghai A-shares in mid-2001 was worth just $49 at the end of 2005. In this market, the fact that the negative demographics arising from the one-child per family policy will, in the short run, be outweighed economically by the huge increase in urbanisation is irrelevant in terms of stockmarket

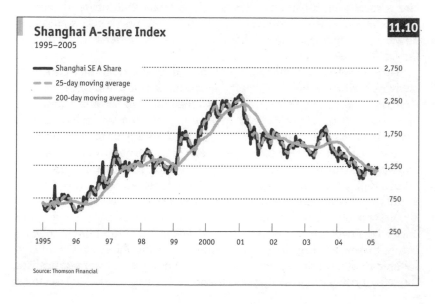

**Shanghai A-share Index**
1995–2005

**11.10**

— Shanghai SE A Share
– – 25-day moving average
— 200-day moving average

Source: Thomson Financial

performance. It is the structural limitations that have had by far the most influence on the market. As can been in Figure 11.10 on the previous page, there is little correlation between the Chinese market and the US cycle, particularly after the 2001 peak.

The Beijing government has said that it intends to reduce the government's stake in companies, but it is hard to see how this will be accomplished without creating some disruption in the market. Working out which shares will fare best in a "socialist stockmarket with Chinese characteristics" requires detailed knowledge about not only the companies concerned but also the way the market as a whole operates. Some fund managers are sufficiently knowledgeable to be able to cherry pick their way through Chinese stocks, but many firms selling investment products linked to China's stockmarket will not have the necessary expertise. Investors seeking to ride on the coat-tails of the Chinese dragon should either try to find a good specialist fund or invest in international companies that are beneficiaries of the growth trend.

## India

India has a well-established stockmarket with many more quoted companies than China and shares are allowed to trade freely. But its main advantage compared with China is that it is a democracy, and this political flexibility may make it easier to negotiate the challenges that inevitably face a society in transition. Allowing for the fact that during the 1990s India was on a broadly sideways road map whereas the US was on an upward-sloping one, India has been following the underlying rhythm of the US four-year cycle.

An analysis of the performance of the Indian stockmarket shows how studying charts can help to identify when markets are undergoing major changes in trend. The Sensex index hit a high of 4,546 on March 2nd 1992 and over three consecutive cycles of four years the market traded broadly sideways. The cycle that started in 1998 reached a new high of 6,150 in 2000 (this peak is not evident in Figure 11.11 as the figures are rounded), and although the market subsequently retreated, the move through 4,500 (which defined the upper parameter of the sideways trend) was the first signal that the market might be about to move into a secular uptrend.

Even powerful secular trends do not move in a straight line and, influenced by developments in the United States, some pull-back is likely before the next four-year cycle gets under way. But the Indian market is in the grip of a secular uptrend and history shows that, once established, the rate of rise is remarkably persistent.

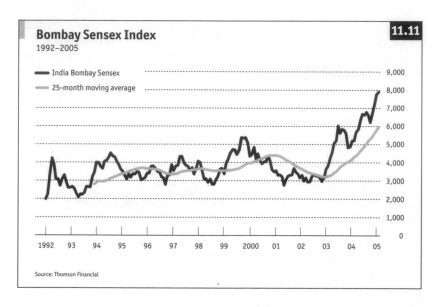

**Bombay Sensex Index**
1992–2005

`11.11`

— India Bombay Sensex
— 25-month moving average

9,000
8,000
7,000
6,000
5,000
4,000
3,000
2,000
1,000
0

1992  93  94  95  96  97  98  99  2000  01  02  03  04  05

Source: Thomson Financial

Two other factors should give added impetus to the upward phase of the cycle:

- The Indian market will come to represent a growing weighting in the world equity index, which means that global index tracking funds will be forced to ratchet up their exposure to the market, thereby reinforcing the uptrend.
- The rating that the market can sustain in terms of P/E ratio, bolstered by investment in India's infrastructure, will be higher than its current level of 13.8. At this stage, it will probably justify a premium rating compared with other emerging markets.

Markets in strong secular uptrends are prone to investment bubbles similar to that experienced by Japan at the end of its 1980s boom. The most likely period for this to occur in India is 2014–20. During this period it may well be suggested that India is capable of becoming the dominant global economic force (just as some analysts in the 1980s predicted that Japan would overtake the United States). The market will then discount an economic scenario far in excess of what India will actually be able to deliver – which is how all bubbles start – and share prices will rise almost vertically. It is possible that from such an investment bubble India (and some of the other catch-up markets if they have also experi-

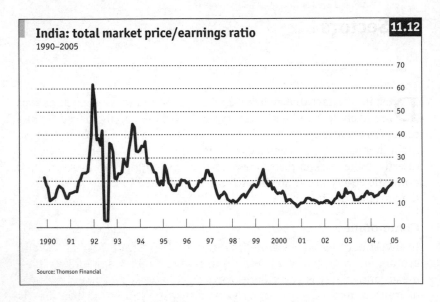

**India: total market price/earnings ratio**
1990–2005

11.12

Source: Thomson Financial

enced speculative bubbles) could follow the same road map as Japan did post-1989. But by then the world will be a radically different place. The problems and political preoccupations of western countries will probably no longer be the dominant force in global economics.

## 12  Sectors

Despite the fact that neither the US nor the European stockmarkets are likely to be in a secular uptrend over the coming decade, some sectors in these markets will do extremely well on the back of the investment themes outlined earlier. Investors who are nervous about investing directly in the stockmarkets of less-developed countries can structure their domestic equity portfolios in such a way that they, too, can benefit from their secular uplift.

### Commodities

In investment terms, commodities are at the forefront of the catch-up economies' march towards industrialisation. China's appetite for base metals and energy is particularly voracious. It is now the largest importer of iron ore and steel. In 2000, it imported 70m tonnes of iron ore. By 2004, the figure had almost trebled to 208m tonnes. In 2005, its imports of stainless steel – 2.9m tonnes – were more than double those of France, the second largest stainless steel importer. By 2030, it will match the United States in oil imports.

Demand for raw materials from the catch-up economies is likely to

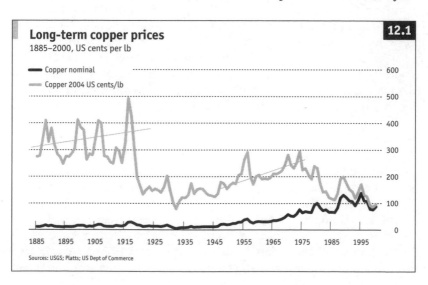

**Long-term copper prices**

1885–2000, US cents per lb

— Copper nominal
— Copper 2004 US cents/lb

Sources: USGS; Platts; US Dept of Commerce

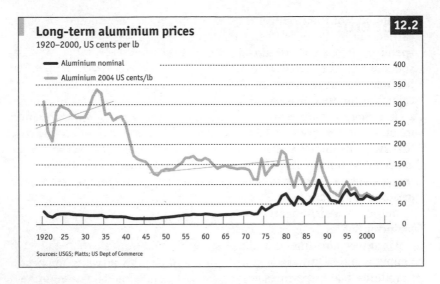

**Long-term aluminium prices**
1920–2000, US cents per lb

■ Aluminium nominal
■ Aluminium 2004 US cents/lb

Sources: USGS; Platts; US Dept of Commerce

trigger another "supercycle" in the commodity markets that could well last for several decades. As Figure 12.1 on the previous page shows, there have been two such previous cycles: one from the late 1880s to the early 1900s and the other from 1945 to 1975. The first was driven by the industrialisation of the US while the second was initially triggered by the post-war reconstruction of Europe in the aftermath of the Second World War and was then given an additional boost by Japan's rapid economic growth.

Even in a supercycle, prices do not go up in a straight line. The smooth curvilinear lines of a theoretical supply-and-demand graph belie the stutters and time lags by which an equilibrium price level is achieved. There will be periods when supply pushes ahead of even the huge demand coming from China and India, and at such times prices will drop sharply. But the underlying trend will be upwards.

## Luxury goods

Agrarian economies usually have an unequal distribution of wealth. As industrialisation gathers momentum, a middle class gradually emerges. Rising per-head income allows people to spend some of their wealth on non-essential goods.

Travel and luxury goods are likely to be prime beneficiaries of rising per-head incomes. In 2004, 28m Chinese people travelled abroad, and the World Tourism Organisation estimates that by 2015 this figure will have risen to 100m. Chinese tourists generally stay in inexpensive hotels and devote 90% of their budget to product shopping. According to research carried out by Chinese Interactive Media Group, with an average daily spend of $175, they are already moving up the league table of high-spending tourists. Anxious to capitalise on this fast-growing trend, many big hotel and travel companies are gearing themselves up to cater specifically for Chinese tourists.

In many catch-up economies the concept of luxury is linked predominantly with conspicuous consumption and enhancing social status. The luxury goods industry is in its infancy in China and its development is expected to mirror that of Japan in the 1980s (in terms of the Chinese market, a luxury good is defined as any item costing more than Rmb5,000 or $625). At that time, when travelling abroad, the Japanese also used to spend 90% of their budget on exclusive products, but they are now spending an increasing amount on expensive hotels, restaurants and concerts.

Until recently, limited availability in their home markets meant that people living in China and India had to go abroad to buy their luxury goods, but all the big fashion designers now have shops in Delhi, Beijing and Shanghai (the Armani shop in Shanghai, for example, is its second largest in the world). By 2015, it is estimated that around $11.5 billion will be spent in China on luxury goods – a quarter of the global market – as 175m people move into the income bracket that will allow them to buy these goods.

## Biotechnology

Pharmaceuticals and biotechnology companies will be the most obvious beneficiaries of the biotechnological revolution as a result of demand from three primary sources:

- new treatments for illnesses or conditions for which there is no existing remedy;
- increasing longevity and therefore more treatments for age-related conditions such as Alzheimer's disease;
- rising prosperity in the developing world which will lead, as it has in the developed world, to more emphasis on health care.

Biotechnology and software companies involved in successful innovations could see their share prices rise spectacularly almost overnight. But again, spotting companies that are incubating new innovations requires specialised knowledge. The majority of investors will secure superior returns by investing in companies that can harness the overall rise in demand for medical treatment.

# Conclusion

The underlying rhythm of the business cycle defines the broad trend of the stockmarket. Powered by two human characteristics – greed and fear – the stockmarket oscillates around the underlying economic trend in a series of clearly defined cycles. Thus even in the financial markets history repeats itself. In the introduction to a 1995 reprint of Charles Mackay's book *Extraordinary Popular Delusion and the Madness of Crowds* (first published in 1841), Norman Stone, an academic, noted: "Parallels may be found today for almost every chapter heading." Since Stone wrote that introduction the internet bubble can be added to the long list of speculative manias which can be traced back to the Mississippi Scheme, the South Sea Bubble and Tulipmania. The repetition is not always exact but the characteristics are the same and cycle analysis picks them up. It provides investors with a financial "compass" – by pointing them in the right broad direction.

In trying to identify which sector or share within a particular market is likely to show outperformance, an investor is trying to pick the winners and losers in Schumpeter's process of "creative destruction". A visual representation of this process can be seen in a chart of a share price, as it is the new, dynamic industries that are the growth stocks. By setting stock selection within the context of cycle analysis, investors will know whether it is appropriate to chase momentum or pursue a more defensive strategy.

## The changing economic landscape

In the decades ahead investors must adapt their portfolios to the changing economic landscape. There is nothing new in the processes of industrialisation and innovation. As Figure 12.1 on page 117 shows, commodity prices rose sharply in response to previous periods of industrialisation, and the discovery of radio, which extended communication from the printed word to the airwaves, prompted the same excitement as the internet has today. Even the cycle of prosperity shifting back to the East is not new. As recently as 1820, the two largest economies in the world were China and India. Together they accounted for about half of global GDP. Then came the Industrial Revolution, which tilted the economic balance in favour of the West. It created incredible wealth in Europe and later the

United States, but at the same time the East seemed to slip backwards and enter a more primitive era. Despite their huge land masses and populations, both China and India declined and became small, introspective economies. As a result, they were trapped in prolonged secular downtrends as far as investment opportunities were concerned. The pendulum is now swinging in the opposite direction.

The transition from an agrarian-based economy to an industrialised one is difficult, and in the case of China there is the additional complication of moving away from a command economy to a more market-oriented one. There are bound to be problems, and countries can trip up badly as they try to negotiate their way along the path towards industrialisation. But between them China and India should provide the sort of global economic thrust that was experienced when the G7 group of industralised countries underwent a similar process.

The developed economies face their own problems in assimilating this transition. There is a risk that the pressures of adjusting to the new economic order against a background of large global imbalances will precipitate a downturn. It is always easier to manage a period of change when the background economic factors are in equilibrium, but the presence of imbalances does not necessarily presage a financial crisis.

## Political challenges

The catalyst for any shock to the financial system may not be economic; there are a large number of political hurdles that must be negotiated during this period of economic change.

After the war in Iraq and, before that, Vietnam, the United States risks becoming more insular, and reluctance to engage in external affairs may blind Americans to the changing economic landscape outside their country. Free trade is essential for the process of globalisation, and the lack of progress of the Doha trade negotiations does not augur well for further liberalisation of trade policy.

Sharing the role of being the economic engine for the world economy could also present some political challenges for the United States, since the increasing economic power of the East brings with it greater political power. In the past, American governments have expressed frustration that Europe has not become more of a global power in economic and political terms. But the rejection of the European Constitution by the French and Dutch has taken the wind out of Europe's political sails. It is much more likely that China will step up to assume the role of "junior" superpower. This will create a political quandary for the United States, which sees

China as a threat, and it is far from certain that Americans will be keen to share or, looking even further ahead, concede the role of number one superpower to China. If the United States is forced to share its superpower status, India would be the preferred partner, but the latter still lags a long way behind China in terms of economic power, although more favourable demographics and a democratic political structure may eventually weigh in India's favour.

## Investment opportunity of the century

At the time this book went to press in mid-2006, stockmarkets had enjoyed a longer than average bull run. Trends do not continue indefinitely and there is likely to be a pause or correction. Given the presence of such large structural imbalances, any downturn is bound to prompt fears of a prolonged recession of the type experienced in Japan. But an analysis of economic cycles and the longer-term themes examined in this book suggest that any such downturn over the next decade will present investors with a once-in-a-century investment opportunity.

The economic catch-up of China, India and other developing countries is the challenge of our age. From an investor's perspective, understanding the underlying cyclical rhythm behind this transition will help to map out the investment opportunities created by the next wave of industrialisation in tomorrow's world.

# Note on sources

The author and the publisher would like to thank all those who gave permission for their material to be used in *Mapping the Markets*. Every effort has been made to trace and acknowledge correctly all copyright material in this book. Any inadvertent errors will, if brought to the attention of the publisher, be corrected in future editions.

# Bibliography

**Introduction**
Dent, H.S., *The Great Boom Ahead*, Hyperion, 1993.

***Part 1 Tools for mapping the markets***
**1 Economic cycles**
Kondratieff, N., *The Long Wave*, Richardson & Snyder, 1984.
Mankiw, N.G., *Macroeconomics*, 5th edn, Worth Publishers, 2003.
Jevons, W.S., *Investigations in Currency and Finance*, Macmillan, 1909.
Schumpeter J.A., *Business Cycles: A Theoretical Historical and Statistical Analysis of the Capitalistic Process*, McGraw-Hill, 1939.
Schumpeter, J.A., *Capitalism, Socialism and Democracy*, Counterpoint edn, Unwin Paperbacks, 1987.
Solzhenitsyn, A., *Gulag Archipelago*, vol. 1, Collins, Harvill Press and Fontana, 1976.

**2 Stockmarket cycles**
Bootle, R., *Money for Nothing*, Nicholas Brealey Publishing, 2003.
Hirsch, Y. and Hirsch, J., *Stock Trader's Almanac*, John Wiley & Sons, 2005.
*Investors' Chronicle*, April 30th–May 6th 2004.
Murphy, J.J., *Intermarket Analysis*, John Wiley & Sons, 2004.
Siegel, J.J., *Stocks for the Long Run*, 3rd edn, McGraw-Hill, 2002.

**4 Stock selection**
Mandelbrot, B.B., *The (Mis)Behaviour of Markets*, Profile Books, 2004.
Murphy, J.J., *Technical Analysis of the Futures Markets*, New York Institute of Finance/Prentice-Hall, 1986.
Plummer, A., *Forecasting the Financial Markets*, Kogan Page, 1989.
Smith, A., *The Wealth of Nations*, Books I–III, Penguin Classics, 1986.
Prechter, R.R. Jr, *The Major Works of R.N. Elliott*, New Classics Library, 1980.

**Part 3 Long-term cyclical drivers**
**5 Catch-up industrialisation**

Desai, M., *India and China: An Essay in Comparative Political Economy*, IMF Paper for IMF Conference on India/China, Delhi, 2003.

*Foreign Direct Investment in China: Some Lessons for Other Countries*, IMF Discussion Paper PDP/02/3, International Monetary Fund, Washington, DC, February 2002.

*IMF Country Report*, no. 04/351, International Monetary Fund, Washington, DC, 2002.

*IMF Economic Outlook*, International Monetary Fund, Washington, DC, September 2005.

Kochhar, K., Kumar, U., Rajan, R., Subramanian, A. and Tokatlidis, I., *India's Pattern of Development: What Happened, What Follows?*, IMF Working Paper WP/06/22, 2005.

Maddison, A., *Chinese Economic Performance in the Long Run*, Development Centre of the Organisation for Economic Co-operation and Development, Paris, 1998.

*OECD Economic Surveys*, vol. 2005/13, China, OECD Publishing, September 2005.

O'Neill, J., Lawson, S., Wilson, D., Purushothaman, R., Buchanan, M. and Lord Griffiths of Fforestfach, *Growth and Development: The Path to 2050*, Goldman Sachs, 2003.

Prasard, E. (ed.), *China's Growth and Integration into the World Economy; Prospects and Challenges*, IMF Occasional Paper 232, Washington, DC, 2004.

Tseng, W. and Zebregs, H., *Foreign Direct Investment in China: Some Lessons for Other Countries*, IMF Policy Discussion Paper PDP/02/3, 2002.

Walter, C.E. and Howie, F., *Privatising China: the stock markets and their role in corporate reform*, Wiley (Asia), 2003.

**6 Demographics**

Bloom, D.E. and Williamson, J.G., "Demographic Transitions and Economic Miracles in Emerging Asia", *The World Economic Review*, vol. 12, no. 3, September 1998.

Dent, H.S., *The Great Boom Ahead*, Hyperion, 1993.

"How Will Demographic Change Affect the Global Economy?", *World Economic Outlook*, International Monetary Fund, Washington, DC, September 2004.

Modelski, G. (ed.), *Exploring Long Cycles*, Lynne Rienner Publishers, 1987.

Preston, S.H., "Children and the elderly: Divergent paths for America's dependents", *Demography*, vol. 21, 1984.

Strauss, W. and N. Howe, *Generations*, William Morrow, 1991.

*World Population Prospects: The 2002 Revision, Volume I: Comprehensive Tables*, Population Division, Department of Economic and Social Affairs, UN, 2003.

*World Population Prospects: The 2002 Revision, Volume II: Sex and Age*, Population Division, Department of Economic and Social Affairs, UN, 2003.

*World Population Prospects: The 2002 Revision, Volume III: Analytical Report*, Population Division, Department of Economic and Social Affairs, UN, 2003.

## 7 Energy

Lovelock, J., *The Revenge of Gaia*, Allen Lane, 2006.

Santarius, J.F. and Kulcinski, G.L., *Astrofuel: An Energy Source for the 21st Century*, Fusion Technology Institute, University of Wisconsin-Madison, 1989.

## 8 Biotechnology

"Biotechnology", *Financial Times Survey*, November 27th 2001.

*BMJ*, November 5th 2005.

Haggard, H.W., *Devils, Drugs and Doctors: The Story of the Science of Healing from Medicine-man to Doctor*, Pocket Books Inc, 1946.

For a detailed discussion of developments in nanorobotics see www. nanotech-now.com/products/nononewsnow/issues/003/003.htm

### Part 3 Downward phases of the cycle
## 9 Global imbalances

Plummer, Tony, "A Theoretical Basis of Technical Analysis", *Market Technician*, no. 54, October 2005.

*The Potential Economic Impact of an Avian Flu Pandemic on Asia*, Asian Development Bank, November 2005. www.adb.org/Documents/ EDRC/Policy_Briefs/PB042.pdf

## 10 Negative shocks

*Asian Development Outlook*, Asian Development Bank, 2006.

The Earth Policy Institute, www.earth-policy.org

"The Global Implications of an Asian Flu Pandemic", *World Economic Outlook*, International Monetary Fund, Washington, DC, April 2006.

*Water for People, Water for Life*, United Nations World Water
    Development Report, UNESO Publishing/Berghahn Books, 2003.

**Part 4 Taking market bearings**
**11 Stockmarkets**

*Evaluating and Comparing the Innovation Performance of the United
    States and the European Union*, European Commission, 2005 (www.
    trendchart.org/scoreboards/scoreboard2005/index/index.cfm).
*Global Economic Outlook*, vol. 1, Capital Economics, 2006.
Graham, B., *The Intelligent Investor*, 4th edn, Harper & Row, 1973.
Okamota, H., "Asset allocation in Japanese and US stock markets by
    means of technical analysis", *Market Technician*, no. 46, March 2003.
Shiller, R.J., *Irrational Exuberance*, Princeton University Press, 2000.

**12 Sectors**

China Interactive Media Group
Rogers, J., *Hot Commodities*, John Wiley & Sons, 2005.

**Conclusion**

Mackay, C., *Extraordinary Popular Delusion and the Madness of Crowds*,
    Wordsworth Editions, 1995.
Maddison, A., *The World Economy: A Millennial Perspective*, The
    Development Centre of the Organisation for Economic Co-Operation
    and Development, Paris, 2001.
US-China Economic and Security Review Commission's Hearing on
    China's Growing Global influence: Objectives and Strategy, July
    21st-22nd 2005. www.uscc.gov/hearings/2005hearings/written_
    testimonies/05_07_21_22wrts/damato_richard_open.pdf

**Further reading**

Alexander, M.A., *Stock Cycles: Why Stocks Won't Beat Money Markets over
    the Next Twenty Years*, Writers Club Press, 2000.
Alexander, M.A., *Cycles in American Politics*, iUniverse, 2004.
Dent, H.S. Jr, *The Next Great Bubble Boom*, Free Press, 2006.
Sterling, W.P. and Waite, S.R., *Boomernomics: The Future of Your Money in
    the Upcoming Generational Warfare*, Ballantine Books, 1998.

# Index